Teddy Tales

Bears Repeating, Too!

By Terry & Doris Michaud

Illustrations by Thomas J. Mocny
unless otherwise credited

Published by Hobby House Press   Cumberland,
Maryland 21502

Additional Copies of this book may be purchased at $19.95
from
HOBBY HOUSE PRESS, INC.
900 Frederick Street
Cumberland, Maryland 21502
or from your favorite bookstore or dealer.
Please add $2.25 per copy postage.

Printed in the United States of America

ISBN: 0-87588-349-4

Table of Contents

Dedication

This book is dedicated to our grandchildren, Geni Rae Michaud, Joshua Messinger, Melissa Baese, Molly Messinger and Abby Michaud. They have added an immeasurable dimension of love to our lives that will take us a lifetime to repay.

Acknowledgements

The quality of any book is greatly enhanced by the quality of the photography. We are indeed fortunate to be able to work with an outstanding professional and good friend, Tom Mocny. Gary Ruddell, Carolyn Cook and all of the good folks at Hobby House Press, Inc., make it possible for us to share our stories with you. Additional assistance was gratefully accepted from Paul and Rosemary Volpp, Donna Harrison, Dottie Ayers, Wayne Bush, Al Stratton, Barbara Wolters, Linda Kuhn, Kathy Thomas, Beth Savino, Barbara and Bob Lauver and Dwight and Dorothy Austin. We also wish to thank the many store owners and managers who have been of immense assistance, the hundreds of artists and bear makers, and the thousands of collectors who are so important in our lives. There are countless others whose names are not mentioned but are equally as important. Last, but not least, we wish to thank Bill and Rosemary Hayes, close friends and business associates who share our enthusiasm and love for teddy bears and arctophiles.

The Professor — An Overview

The Professor, 18in (46cm), mascot and spokesbear for the Carrousel Museum Collection.

Since the writing of our two previous books, *Bears Repeating, Stories Old Teddy Bears Tell* and *How To Make and Sell Quality Teddy Bears*, a lot of wonderful things have happened to us. Our business has continued to flourish and grow, and we have met many more marvelous teddy bear collectors all around the United States. The Professor has continued to travel from coast to coast and introduce us to a host of arctophiles from many walks of life, all with the same love of the teddy bear.

One new direction we have been able to take is to reach many additional collectors through our regular column "Bears Repeating" in *Teddy Bear and friends*® magazine. It has always given us great pleasure to share stories of some of the teddy bears that have come into our collection. That

pleasure is amplified when we can share stories of some of the teddies and their owners that we have had the pleasure to meet in the past few years (see Section II). Some of the stories touch your funny bone and others touch the heart, but all are real stories about real people and their very real teddy bears.

Another new direction our handcrafted teddy bears have taken can be found half way around the world in the exciting country of Australia. Perth is the home of a marvelous teddy bear shop called The Twig. The manager of this shop inquired about handling our teddy bears for her growing collector trade. We made arrangements to ship bears by ground transportation due to the high cost of air shipments to Australia. The teddies were apparently met with great enthusiasm by her customers because she informed us that the first few shipments were sold within days of their arrival.

The Professor strikes up a happy relationship with his new friend, Mickey.

Carrousel by Michaud teddy bears are traveling far and wide. One of their favorite destinations is Australia.

Selling American artists' bears in Australia, as in foreign countries, adds greatly to their cost due to shipping and duty that must be paid. This makes us even more proud to have our product represented there.

We recently completed arrangements to have our teddy bears offered in a shop called Enchanted Bears located near Melbourne. Joy Christopher is the charming owner and a delight to do business with. We get regular reports on the growing Australian collector's market from David Worland, one of Australia's advanced teddy bear collectors and a frequent visitor to the States.

Teddy bears have been winning the hearts of young and old alike since they came into being just after the turn of the century. They have reportedly won top sales honors during the holiday season year after year, almost since their inception. We suspect those sales numbers are appropriately strong the rest of the year as well.

There is, however, a strong contender for nearly the same degree of popularity as the teddy bear. It is instantly recognized around the world and his devoted followers are legend. His name is Mickey Mouse, created by Walt Disney in 1928. A large family of Disney characters has evolved since then, but the center of attention always comes back to Mickey. Licensed products have found their way into collections everywhere, and Mickey and his friends have starred in cartoons and feature length films that have been enjoyed by children of all ages. The Disneyland and Disney World theme parks annually draw millions of visitors to their respective locations in California and Florida. In short, mention the word Disney or Mickey Mouse and it starts a warm glow inside you that compares favorably to the feeling of discovering yet another teddy bear for the collection.

Having been struck by the Disney charm as a child (an inner glow that has never really subsided), you can imagine our delight when we first heard that the Disney people in Florida were making plans to hold their very first Teddy Bear Convention! That delight was heightened when we were invited to participate. What a perfect combination — Mickey Mouse and the teddy bear! A great deal of time and effort was spent by some of the top people from a variety of departments at Walt Disney World in Florida. A December date in 1988 was selected and a full scale plan was put in motion. I must admit we had some misgivings about a December date, feeling that it might be difficult to entice people to include the convention in their holiday plans. I should have recognized that when you combine the charm of the teddy bear with the excitement of Mickey Mouse and friends, it is a combination that just cannot miss.

The Disney team, headed by executive Wayne Bush, not only enlisted the help of the many talents within their organization, but they consulted early with leading authorities from a number of areas of expertise in the "Teddy Bear World." Gary Ruddell, publisher of *Teddy Bear and friends* magazine, and Peter Kalinke, representative of the world famous Gebrüder Hermann teddy bear firm in Germany were consulted frequently, almost from the conception of the idea. Key people from Walt Disney World attended the fall 1987 Baltimore convention and show where they were able to see first hand what goes into putting on one of the top conventions in the country. It was at this convention that we were asked to be among the featured guests at their convention.

Since our winter personal appearance tour included Florida, we were invited to exhibit our handcrafted teddy bears in the gift shop of the American Adventure pavilion in Epcot Center during our 1988 tour. The success of this visit led to a return showing during our 1989 tour.

I will not take the time or space here to give you a detailed, hour by hour report of the convention, but I can tell you that it was an unqualified resounding success. All of the Disney people involved were pleased, the number of guests were pleased and most importantly, the hundreds of guests who attended went away with a firm resolve to return for the Second Annual Walt Disney World® Teddy Bear Convention. A Disney artist perfectly captured the warm feeling everyone felt and reflected it in his convention logo drawing of Mickey Mouse cuddling a teddy bear.

Having learned many years ago that you cannot stand still in business, you either move forward or slide backward, we have made an effort to continue a good deal of planning and developing, not only in our current lines, but in new areas as well. We do not seem to have any shortage of ideas to develop, but rather a shortage of time to develop the ideas we already have.

Without tipping our hat full of ideas, I can assure you that you will see the Carrousel by Michaud name come up in some interesting and we think unique areas that have yet to be explored. Whatever success we have achieved to date, and no matter what new directions we may follow, let us give credit where credit is due. This success just simply would not have happened without you, the collector and you, the retailer, and yes, you, the teddy bear artists and manufacturers. We have gained much from each and every one of you. It is the warm feeling that passes from each new teddy bear arctophile we meet, directly into our being that keeps us challenged and keeps that burning desire aglow to continue sharing with all of you.

Aunt Eunice

10in (25cm) teddy bear acquired from the original owner, with photograph of owner as a child.

We are occasionally asked how we find so many unique and unusual antique teddy bears for our museum collection, particularly those with stories behind them. I am sure that more than one or two people believe that because we are so well known in teddy bear circles, that most, if not all of the bears in our collection have been brought to us by owners who are delighted to have their teddy become part of our famous collection.

Let me assure you that by and large, most of the teddy bears in our collection have come to us the same way they come to the rest of you...by seeking them out everywhere we go. First, you must recognize that we have been collecting teddy bears since the early 1970s. The hobby quickly went from a collection to an addiction. We were operating an antique business at the time, specializing in toys and dolls, and had built a friendship among a rather large circle of antique dealers that we did shows with. Recognize also that in those days there was very little demand for the fuzzy creatures we have grown to love, so it was reasonably easy to find them, and prices were relatively low, although it did not seem like it at the time.

We had no idea at the time why we were putting a great deal of effort into building our collection. Certainly we were unaware that it was to become a vital part of our business. I even made the statement on one occasion to Doris, "Don't you tell any of my friends I paid a hundred dollars for a teddy bear. They don't think I'm too tightly wrapped as it is."

Now that we have carefully explained that our collection

Aunt Eunice (right) with her sister.

Aunt Eunice was born in 1910 and grew up in a small Southwestern Michigan community. The teddy bear was purchased in 1912 at the General Store where area farmers, lumbermen and furniture makers came to buy supplies. The combined grocery and dry goods store was well stocked with practical merchandise, including barrels of flour, brown sugar, maple syrup and other basic supplies for the family cook. Mother might also find some attractive, reasonably priced bolts of fabric that she could use to put her sewing skills to work. Dad could find plenty to fill his needs as well, including basic tools, harness and other needs for the horses, and perhaps some chewing tobacco. Precious few items of luxury were to be found at the country store because people from that era were frugal by necessity. There were a limited number of goods that would more properly be placed on a "want" list, rather than a "need" list, such as cast iron banks for boys and china dolls for little girls. Teddy bears were a relatively new toy at that time but you can be sure that a well-stocked store would have at least one or two teddy bears for the young trade.

Doris turned her attention to cleaning and repairing the teddy bear. More often than not the teddy bears we find are sans clothing or any type of decor. While we rarely have a desire to create elaborate costumes for our bears, we do frequently feel that a small touch of costuming might enhance his or her character. Such was the case with Aunt Eunice's bear. It somehow seemed appropriate to put a delicate antique lace collar on her teddy, fastened in the front with a small piece of costume jewelery we frequently acquire for just such a purpose.

The teddy found a spot in our showcases, nestled in with several other bears of his size and age.

Now we move the calendar ahead about one year. Through our door came a tall pleasant lady with snow white hair. Without taking time to look through the shop, she approached Doris and said that her nephew had sold us a small teddy bear a while ago and she wondered what had become of it. Doris smiled and said "Why, you must be Aunt Eunice! Come and see your bear." As soon as she spotted her teddy in the showcase, a smile of relief and pleasant surprise crossed her face. She was pleased to find out that her teddy was not cast aside as she feared it might be. She was also pleased to find that it had been cleaned and repaired.

Opening her purse, she pulled out an old photograph taken of herself and her sister as children. "I thought you might like to have this old photo to keep with the bear." Now it was our turn to wear the smile of pleasant surprise. We have named the bear "Aunt Eunice," and she is always displayed with the photograph of her original owner.

Aunt Eunice's teddy bear, circa 1912.

grew basically the same way most collections do, a teddy or two at a time through a lot of searching and looking, let me admit that there have been an occasional bear that has come our way through no effort on our part, but simply by being in the right place at the right time. We tell just about anyone who will listen that we collect teddy bears and sooner or later, the word is going to reach someone who has a bear that they want to part with, either for monetary reasons, or because they truly want to find a good home for it. In some instances it may be a combination of both reasons.

At any rate, we do have some very special teddy bears that now reside in our collection that have come to us from the original owner. One such teddy came through our front door inside a paper bag carried by a gentleman of middle age. I realize the term "middle age" is rather subjective, but let us just say he was some where near my age. "I understand you folks like teddy bears" he said, pulling a small 10in (25cm) rather decrepit teddy from the bag. "My Aunt Eunice is moving to Florida and she asked me to find somebody that might want it."

The bear was truly in need of repair but it had several redeeming features about it, including the fact that it came from the original owner. It also had an expression on the face that can best be described as a smirk. A price was agreed upon and we then began to ask questions. Who is Aunt Eunice? Where did she grow up? Did the teddy have a special name? I am sure that people must at times feel like we are giving them the third degree, but I can tell you that some small fact that seems almost insignificant to someone can lead to a delightful story about the owner or the teddy bear.

Northern Michigan Bears

20in (51cm) American teddy, circa 1920s, obtained in Mackinac City, Michigan.

British teddy from 1930s, given to Doris by original owner Wayne Wilson.

1930s teddy found in California that closely resembles Doris' childhood teddy bear.

Our tale of three Northern Michigan bears begins appropriately at Mackinaw City, which adjoins the Straits of Mackinaw, that body of water that separates Michigan into two very distinct land masses, the Upper and Lower Peninsula. Geography was never my strong suit in school but I believe that Michigan is the only state in the nation that is divided into two parts. The two land masses are now connected by the Mackinaw bridge, spanning the Straits with an engineering miracle that exceeds five miles. The bridge is a tourist attraction all by itself, but the whole area is steeped in history and Indian lore that regularly draws tourists from thousands of miles.

Before the bridge was constructed in the 1950s, access to the Upper and Lower Peninsulas was accomplished by ferry boats. Not just ordinary boats, these ships actually carried great numbers of automobiles at regular intervals from one side to the other. During the summer high tourist season and again during hunting season in the late fall, cars would be lined up for miles, waiting their turn to board one of several car ferries. Sometimes that wait could run into hours. The bridge has certainly eliminated that bottleneck, but the experience of crossing the Straights by car ferry is one that will be cherished forever.

The Great Lakes surrounding Michigan are heavy in the lore of shipping because, for many years it was the primary means of moving goods from one end of the state to the other. All types of merchandise was loaded onto steamships and sent on its way up and down the five lakes comprising the Great Lakes. One such line that regularly carried goods from Detroit to Mackinaw was the Detroit and Cleveland Steamship Lines. We know of at least one teddy bear that made the voyage from the port of Detroit to find a home in St. Ignace, a small community in Michigan's upper peninsula just across the bridge from Mackinaw City.

The teddy came to our attention in 1981 when we were showing our antique teddies at the Voyageur Shop in Mackinaw City. A story in an area newspaper prompted an elderly couple to bring the bear into the shop. The teddy, an American bear from the mid 1920s, was in better than average condition. Teddy bears that can trace their origins to the United States do not generally command the kinds of high prices that those of German ancestry do but we are always delighted to find good quality American teddies, not only because they are more directly connected to our heritage, but we feel that prices of good American bears are going to appreciate rather well in the coming years. After all, there

13

Northern Michigan bears on permanent hibernation in the Carrousel Museum.

were fewer American teddy bears made when you compare their production figures to those of Steiff and other German producers.

We were not able to get a detailed history of this excellent teddy because it belonged to another member of the family than the one that brought it to us, but you can be sure it found a welcome spot in our collection.

For the story of our second Northern Michigan bear, we move down the Lower Peninsula to Alpena, Michigan, where a young lad named Wayne Wilson was born and raised. To be more specific, Wayne lived on the French road in an area that was known to locals as Silver City. The small community was not a city in the classic sense, having no shopping district or city hall, but was an area of private residences on the outskirts of Alpena where people who preferred to live in the country could build a home. A one-room schoolhouse called Case School served the educational needs of grades one through eight. Wayne Wilson attended this school in the 1930s. His teddy, a 15in (38cm) bear that appears to be of English origin, was offered to Doris

about ten years ago at Fashion Square Mall in Saginaw, Michigan, at an antique show we were set up at. The teddy has very special significance to us because Wayne and Doris were schoolmates at Case School in Silver City. Wayne was a few years younger than Doris but remember that the school taught grades one through eight, and all in the same room!

Doris has a lot of fond memories of her youth in Silver City. One memory recalls a small teddy bear that was her constant companion. Many happy hours were spent taking costume jewelry from her mother's jewelry box and draping it around her teddy. Over the course of the years, this bear was lost to future generations but a close replacement was found at a teddy bear show in California. When found, it had no eyes, but that problem was quickly resolved.

Several years ago Doris' mother was preparing to move into an apartment and she asked Doris if she wanted the old jewelry box. She did, indeed, and while rummaging through it, she discovered the glass eye from her childhood teddy bear! The eye has since been placed in the bear from California.

Minocqua

22in (56cm) teddy discovered in Northern Wisconsin during an unplanned detour.

Minneapolis, Minnesota, is the focal point for one of the first teddy bear conventions ever held in the United States. The convention is sponsored by *The Teddy Tribune*, one of the first publications to focus on the arctophiles of the world. The magazine and convention are the brainchild of Barbara Wolters, who is actually a lovable teddy bear in people disguise. Barbara has managed to round up a host of volunteers who labor endless hours to put on a fun-filled, exciting convention every summer.

We have a perfect attendance record at the Teddy Tribune Convention and we keep going back, year after year, because it gives us the opportunity to renew our acquaintance with a wide circle of teddy bear collectors who are loyal participants of this convention. The weather does not always cooperate with those attending the convention and after a bad experience flying through a thunderstorm one year, we have since opted to drive from Michigan, a rather pleasant two-day drive each way. Our path usually takes us

through Michigan's upper peninsula, then across Wisconsin and Minnesota. This not only avoids the traffic congestion around Chicago, but also provides us with some of Michigan's most spectacular scenery.

Our 1988 trip went well during the first day's travel, bringing us to Rhinelander, Wisconsin, where we spent the night. The weather back in Chesaning had been rather warm (in fact 1988 was the year of hot weather all over the country) so we were pleased to experience a pleasant temperature drop as we drove through Michigan's north country and portions of Wisconsin.

We were up and on the road bright and early on a Friday morning, determined to meet our schedule which would get us to Minneapolis in early afternoon, giving us an opportunity to get settled in before our scheduled presentation at the convention. We confirmed highway directions with the waitress at breakfast and headed merrily down the road.

Normally, when we travel, I am occupied with getting us

to our destination and Doris is usually busy doing finish work on yet another teddy bear. Since we were going to do a presentation that afternoon, we chose to take the opportunity of discussing our talk as we traveled.

Doris broke into my conversation with an astonished "Island City!" exclamation as she reached for the road map. I glanced up to see an unfamiliar highway number and a sign that said, "Welcome to Minocqua, Wisconsin." By now the traffic was building up as we entered the town, and we drove another few miles into the community before we opted to pull into a service station for gas and for a review of the road map.

Much to our dismay, we discovered we had driven 50 miles out of our way. We searched the map for an alternate route to get us back toward Minneapolis but as luck would have it, the shortest route was right back to where we had taken a wrong turn. This meant we were going to be at least two hours late, so we pulled back onto the road and headed back over the same territory we had just covered. As we approached an intersection in Minocqua, we saw a roadside sign that gave directions to an antique show at the local high school. A quick conference led to the agreement that since the high school was just a block away, we would make a quick trip to the antique show and not lose more than 15 minutes or so.

We were dismayed to find out the show was scheduled to open at 10 a.m. and it was now 9 a.m. Without needing to discuss it, we got back on the road. Silence was the rule as we proceeded back in our former direction. About ten miles

from town we glanced at each other, smiled and turned the car around. Without the need to voice it, we both had decided that after all the trouble we had been to, there just had to be a teddy bear waiting for us at that show. Our 30-minute wait in their parking lot gave us ample time to complete our discussion about our presentation at the convention and to come up with one or two excuses for being late!

The antique show was a typical show held in small communities, made up of dealers from perhaps a 100-mile radius of Minocqua. We discovered to our dismay that the show was not just antiques, but also heavily oriented toward crafts, a practice that unfortunately seems to be on the rise around the country. Since there were approximately 20 dealers in the show, it would not take long to quickly pass through. The dealers who did have antiques seemed to be strongly stocked with glassware and furniture.

We had just about resigned ourselves to the fact that our intuition had led us astray, when we entered the next to the last booth in the show. There, sitting in a little red chair was the object of our search. A charming 22in (56cm) teddy, circa 1935, was waiting for us. He seemed to be saying, "Where have you been? I was beginning to think you weren't coming." The dealer was as attracted to the teddy as we were, or so her price indicated, but at this point there was no turning back. Doris busied herself doing some minor repair as we headed for Minneapolis so we would have a new teddy to add to our "Show and Tell" program.

Mississippi Ralph

Our annual winter personal appearance tour takes us from the West Coast, back through Arizona, Texas, into Florida and ending in Tennessee. During the course of our tour, we exhibit many of our antique teddy bears from our museum collection, autograph our books and present our line of handcrafted teddy bears. We do these exhibits in some of the fine shops that handle our handcrafted teddy bears. In this manner, we get to meet firsthand the collectors who have been buying our teddies. It is really the part of the business that we find most rewarding.

We always enjoy our visit to Texas because it gives us a chance to enjoy some of that delightful Texas Barbeque and Bluebell Ice Cream. When our son lived in Texas several years ago, he introduced us to both culinary delights and we have been devotees ever since. Another pleasant part of our tour is renewing our acquaintance with the many store owner friends we have met and worked with since our tours began in 1984. Dolores and Bob Buntz, owners of the Luggage Loft and Bear Corner in Tyler, Texas, are prime examples of the store owners who go out of their way to make our visit a pleasant one. They have even taken us to some of the antique dealers in their area so we can look for antique teddy bears. On one occasion they took us to Canton, Texas, and introduced us to the largest outdoor antique market we have ever been to. It is called "First Monday" because it originally was held on the first Monday of each month. Due to its popularity, it has grown to include the previous three days, with activity now starting on the Thursday before the first Monday. If that sounds a little confusing, it is, but if you have any interest in antiques, this market has something for everyone, including arctophiles. It was at this market that we first met Sally and Jim Stearns, the artists who make those delightfully creative *Stearnsy Bears.*

In 1987 we had a teddy bear seek us out in Tyler. Actually, an older couple brought the bear to us at the Luggage Loft because they saw us on a local television program. The lady showed us the 14in (36cm) American teddy and explained that it belonged to her first husband. Since she was now remarried, the teddy was no longer a family heirloom so she was willing to sell it.

After purchasing the teddy bear, we learned that her first husband's name was Ralph and he grew up in Mississippi. He got the bear around 1920. It seemed appropriate to name the bear "Mississippi Ralph." With that name, it was also deemed fitting to outfit him in a riverboat gambler's vest. This teddy is going to have some tall tales to tell his friends in the Carrousel Museum Collection.

14in (36cm) teddy from Mississippi, circa 1920.

Mississippi Ralph yearns for the good old days spent on his river boat.

A Pair of Clarences

Clarence Morgan's teddy, circa 1920s, 23in (58cm).

It is, without question, a thrill to walk into an antique shop, discover an early Steiff teddy bear lying on a shelf in the back, and even more of a thrill to discover that it is marked at a reasonable price. But we have contended for a number of years now that we are even more thrilled to acquire a teddy bear from the original owner. For one thing, it gives us the opportunity to get a history of the bear and some background information on the owner. Rarely does the antique dealer know any of the history of a given teddy. We also feel rather privileged when an owner entrusts us with something that has been as close to him as a teddy bear has.

How do you find original owner teddy bears? Following the Classified Ads' Antique section in your area newspapers may lead to a teddy in a household sale but this is a rare happening. I go back to a suggestion we make over and over again and that is to tell everybody that you collect teddy bears. As you read the stories about the original owner teddy bears in this and our first book, you can conclude that original

Clarence Cummings' teddy from 1930s, 14in (36cm).

preemie at birth). We have been asked why we have not replaced the eyes with glass eyes like the originals, but we feel the buttons are part of this teddy's charm and he has every right to keep them.

Our second Clarence teddy was a more recent acquisition, coming to us at the Toledo Doll and Teddy Bear Show in 1976. This show, sponsored by the Hobby Center Toys organization, is one of the largest in the country. It is an annual event every fall and features the leading producers from both the doll and teddy bear world. Beth Savino and her family always do an outstanding job in organizing this show that has become a must for collectors from every part of the country.

There are always a number of experts on hand to do authentic appraisals on dolls and teddy bears. Clarence Cummings had brought his teddy in and after it was appraised, he brought his teddy to show us. Doris was immediately taken with it because it was very much like her first teddy bear. He was impressed with the appraised value of his teddy but he seemed more interested in finding a home for it where he knew it would be shared. After a consultation with his family, he decided that he would be pleased to have it become a part of our collection. It is displayed in our showcase with a tag that reads, "Clarence Cummings Teddy Bear."

owners seem to find us. That is true, but if you follow that another step and ask them why they brought the bear to us, in most cases a friend or a relative of theirs told them about our collection. The friend or relative may just have been someone we had occasion to tell about our interest in teddy bears.

Clarence Morgan brought his teddy bear to us about ten years ago at an antique show in Flint, Michigan. His wife had been to the show the first day and saw The Professor (the first teddy in our collection) holding a sign that read "Wanted — Old Teddy Bears." He showed up the next day with his bear. It is a 23in (58cm) charmer from the 1920s and it had two unique features that were strong factors in our decision to buy it. First, it had a pair of white buttons sewn where the original eyes would have been. Clarence was not sure when it happened but he was reasonably certain his mother had sewn them on, perhaps after he had pulled an eye out. Secondly, the bear was outfitted in a striped shirt and rose-colored overalls that was an outfit his baby sister wore (a

Two teddies with a common bond, both owned by boys named Clarence.

Pretty Baby, Teddy Baby

The widely sought Steiff Teddy Baby, 3in (8cm).

When we are traveling we keep a close watch on the local papers, particularly the Antiques for Sale category in the classified section. Such a search turned up an antique show in Orlando, Florida, in 1979, where we were on a business trip in my former occupation as an engineer for Dow Corning Corporation. It was wintertime, which is a great season for antique shows in Florida.

A Michigan antique dealer was set up at the show and we spent nearly an hour in her booth talking about our teddy bear collection. A number of customers joined in the conversation and we had a great time discussing our favorite subject. As we bid our friend farewell, she said, "Aren't you interested in the bear?" I could not imagine how we could have missed her teddy, but she pointed him out in her showcase amid a jumble of jewelry and other treasures. At first glance I thought we had discovered a teddy baby in the

rare miniature size but it turned out to be a Steiff Teddyli, complete with original tag. The resemblance to Teddy Baby is not coincidental because it is obvious the head pattern for Teddy Baby was used for Teddyli. The body for Teddyli was made of rubber, which tended to deteriorate over the years. This example was no exception; the arms and hands tended to be shriveled up. In spite of this shortcoming, the original felt pants and cloth shirt were intact and we were most happy to add it to our collection.

We had determined long ago that a Teddy Baby would be a welcome addition to our collection, but we were also not willing or able to pay the extremely high price to which this very desirable teddy had commanded. We felt that if we were to have one, it would come along in good time. It did just that, and at a place we least expected it.

One of the most popular events we have back home in

Teddy Baby head design used on a bear called Teddyli with doll style rubber body.

Chesaning is a bi-annual antique show, where we set up antique dealers on the beautiful lawns of the mansions and Old Home Shops on our boulevard. It brings dealers from several surrounding states and this, in turn, brings crowds of buyers for the three-day event. It is also a very busy time in our shops because the thousands of shoppers not only check all of the antique booths, but also pour into our shops to see what goodies may be lurking there.

During our fall 1987 show, I received a phone call about mid morning from the shop next door and the lady informed me that she had a dealer set up on her lawn that had a teddy bear we might be interested in. Normally, this would start my heart pounding but I had a shop full of customers, with several patiently waiting at the register. "I can't get away right now and Doris isn't here, but I'll tell her as soon as she returns," was my response.

Doris returned within 15 minutes but we were so busy, I completely forgot to relay the message. Several hours passed and during a slow period in the shop, I remembered the call and suggested that if she had time, she might want to go check it out. She returned in a short time with her hands cupped together to conceal her purchase. "This is the bear the lady had. Are you interested?" she said with a wide grin crossing her face. She opened her hands to reveal the long sought Teddy Baby in the smallest size produced. I can tell you that next time (and there will be a next time), I will not be quite so casual in responding to a teddy bear call. Thank goodness the lady was patient enough to wait until we responded. Incidentally, the bear was priced within our budget.

Ma Daniley

Early Schuco teddy with felt pawpads.

Some of Doris' fondest memories of growing up in Alpena, Michigan, are centered around her grandmother, Nora Daniley, lovingly called Ma Daniley by all of her family. This remarkable lady lived to age 96, leaving three daughters, eleven grandchildren, forty-eight great grandchildren and more great great grandchildren than we could recall.

As a youngster, Doris had the opportunity to spend summers at the Daniley cottages at Long Lake, a beautiful summer resort area just ten miles north of Alpena. Days were spent fishing, swimming, playing in the woods and making friends with the children of tourists staying in the

area. In spite of the demands of Ma Daniley's time to keep the cottages clean and supply the needs of the families renting them, she always took time to see to the needs of her visiting grandchildren. This included providing them with delicious strawberry shortcake, sugar cookies, homemade root beer and other treats.

This wise and kind lady passed along many of her strong moral philosophies on life and living to those around her, a legacy her family will always cherish.

In the mid 1970s Ma Daniley prepared to move into a nursing home and she invited the grandchildren to come

Teddy takes a spin in his pincushion roadster. 3in (8cm) teddy bear, circa 1920s.

Fine china touring car with teddy bear passenger.

Another in a series of fine china pieces themed around teddy bears.

over and pick out some sort of memento to remember her by. Doris and I started out to pay Ma Daniley a visit when we saw a yard sale sign and stopped to check it out. Good fortune smiled on us that morning, for laying on a card table was a tiny Schuco teddy bear. We were a bit taken back by the price of $15.00, for teddy bears were not that much in demand in those days, particularly one so tiny. It was an early Schuco with the felt hand and foot paws that were later eliminated by the manufacturer. Our heart outruled our wallet that day (an occurence that has happened all too frequently since) and the Schuco became part of our collection.

At Ma Daniley's home, Doris looked through her china cabinet and chose a small pot metal pincushion roadster that she had always admired. It seemed only natural to remove the pincushion and place the Schuco teddy bear in the roadster. The teddy has remained in his vehicle ever since. The other keepsake that Doris got from her grandmother was a china roadster with a teddy bear figurine behind the wheel. We have since added a similar china piece with a teddy bear and an open purse.

We have had the good fortune of building a teddy bear collection that includes some rare and unusual pieces that would fetch premium prices, but nothing in the collection carries such a wealth of grand memories of a pleasant childhood and a very special lady known to her family as Ma Daniley, as the little Schuco Teddy does.

Guildford

Our travels in search of teddy bears have taken us to most all parts of the United States (we still have a few areas to explore yet) and to Britain on half-a-dozen occasions. We are frequently asked why we do not include Germany, France or any number of other countries in our itinerary. We are not inclined to do the type of travel that takes in nine countries in ten days, preferring to take ample time to explore each area we are in to its fullest. Because we tend to take so much time in a given area, we still feel we have a great deal to see in Britain before moving on to other countries.

The British Isles are of special interest to us from a historical standpoint as well; Doris has done a good deal of research into British royalty. England is also an excellent hunting ground for the antique buff, which goes hand-in-hand in searching for antique teddy bears. Some of the largest antique markets in the world are held weekly in London and throughout Britain.

It is safe to assume that a fair number of the teddies in our extensive collection have come from the British Isles. The earlier trips were more successful in producing teddy bears for our collection than recent trips, although we have always been able to find teddies there. Prices have certainly appreciated there as they have everywhere but if you look long enough and hard enough, you can find teddy bears to add to your collection, no matter where you are.

It has always been interesting to us to recognize the design features of teddy bears that seem to be related to their country of origin. This is especially true of England, where teddy bears have enjoyed a unique appearance through the years. British teddies seem to have a rather broad face with a nose that is not as pronounced as the German counterpart or the American teddy of the same era. English bears have not commanded the higher prices that German teddies have achieved, but they have recently come into their own in regard to increasing value.

You do not have to make the trip to Britain to add British teddies to your collection. If you collect new bears, England's leading teddy bear makers regularly export their product to the United States and you can find them in most of the leading shops here. In fact, their firms are almost always represented by executives from England at most of the larger teddy bear shows. Antique teddy bears have found their way from England to our shores as well. Some of them were shipped as new products many years ago, some have been brought here by antique dealers who make regular trips overseas and some have been carried here by their original owners coming here as children.

15in (38cm) British teddy from 1934. He grew up with his original owner in Guildford, Surrey, in Great Britain.

Teddy enjoys a biscuit treat from home. This delightful British biscuit tin was discovered at the famous Portobello Road Antique Market.

Guildford is a British teddy bear in our collection that we obtained from the original owner who brought it to this country when she was a child. Her teddy is a pre-war bear from 1934. We were introduced to her and the bear at an antique show in Michigan in the late 1970s. She was born and raised in Guildford, Surrey, a charming area that lies between London and the English Channel. One of our previous trips took us to this area, where we spent a week on a 17th century farm.

If you were a child in Britain in the 1930s, there is a good chance that in addition to having a teddy bear, you would also have owned a Golliwog. It was one of the most popular dolls of its time and is eagerly sought by antique doll collectors today. The Golly was found in many children's books as well and more often than not, it was in the company of a teddy bear. Guildford's owner told us that she had a Golly as a child, handmade for her by her mother. She said that although they were commercially produced, many were handmade from a black stocking by loving nannies.

We had the good fortune of meeting two lovely ladies at the 1988 Baltimore convention that know and understand the importance of the Golliwog to British history. This mother-daughter team from the Cleveland area are both artists of extraordinary talent. Linda Kuhn makes some of the nicest miniature teddy bears we have ever seen. Her daughter, Kathy Thomas, collects Golliwogs and makes a

Our British teddy meets an old favorite, the Golly, by American Artist Kathy Thomas.

striking miniature Golly that is a work of art. Both of these ladies are destined to achieve national recognition for their talented work.

We wanted Guildford to feel at home so he now has one of Kathy's miniature Golliwogs as a companion, along with a British biscuit tin and a childhood book about teddy bears and Golliwogs.

British history confirms the long association of the Golliwog and the teddy bear.

Teddy's Friend, the Panda

28in (71cm) straw-stuffed panda, circa 1930s.

Panda by Merrythought, produced in late 1930s to commemorate the birth of a panda at the London Zoo.

The debate rages on. The panda is absolutely not a bear, but rather from the raccoon family, says one expert. "Poppycock," says another expert. "The new thinking is that the panda is most surely a bear." I suppose it depends on who you ask but we take the position that if the panda is not a bear, he is not aware of it, so it is OK to have them in your bear collection. It would be an unusual collection that does not have at least one panda in it. We know of one teddy bear shop in Indiana called "Panda-Monium" that is stocked with an array of pandas as well as teddy bears, due in large part to owner Terri Altherr's addiction to the "black and white bear."

Our Carrousel Museum Collection certainly has an ample share of pandas that make their home with us. By far the largest of our group is a 28in (71cm) mohair panda that is straw stuffed and probably from the 1930s. He was acquired at the Peoria Doll Show in the late 1970s. He may be of American origin but it is one of those mysteries that we have not solved yet.

Our second panda was a fortunate find at the Heart of Texas Teddy Bear Show in Houston in 1987. We were especially pleased to add him to our collection due to his Merrythought label with registration number clearly indicated on the foot. We have been able to identify it through John Axe's book, *The Magic of Merrythought*, published by Hobby House Press, Inc., and this information was confirmed by a representative from Merrythought who was appearing at the famous Toledo Doll and Toy Show. It was produced in the late 1930s to commemorate the birth of the first panda at the London Zoo.

One of our more unusual pandas is of British origin and has a mechanism that allows the mouth to open when the belly is pressed. We believe it to be from the 1940s. Another open-mouth panda in our collection was produced by Steiff and is highly sought by teddy bear collectors, due in part to its unusual small size.

During one of our earlier trips to Britain in the late 1970s, we were fortunate enough to acquire a complete box of miniature Schuco teddy bears from a small doll store. Since they were all the same color, we traded several of them for Schucos of other colors, and included in our trade was a 3½in (9cm) Schuco panda which is more difficult to find than the other Schuco teddies.

Famed miniaturist Dickie Harrison of Baltimore found out that Doris has a special fondness for pandas and since we have a number of Dickie's miniature teddies in our collection, she made a special panda for us, which is one of our cherished possessions.

While our Carrousel Museum Collection is not focused on a particular part of the teddy bear world, we do seem to favor miniature teddy bears, partly because they do not take up nearly as much room, and partly because we know what effort goes into making regular size teddy bears, which puts us in awe of the miniature makers. One of the most talented of the miniature bear artists is Sarah Phillips from the Baltimore area. She, too, knew of our fondness for pandas and created a very unique bear in her plush medium, then produced a miniature Carrousel Bear in clay for panda to ride on. It has a special place of honor in our collection.

These are by no means the only pandas in our collection, but certainly some of the more interesting of this cuddly creature that has won the hearts of arctophiles all over the world.

Unusual open-mouth panda 14in (36cm).

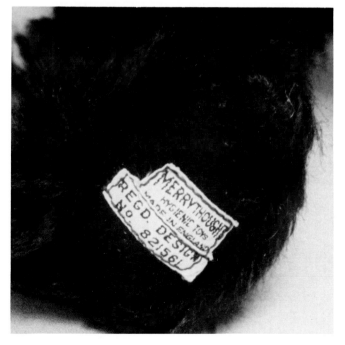

Merrythought panda identified with foot label.

6in (15cm) open-mouth panda by Steiff.

Our tiniest Panda, 2½in (6cm), by American Artist Sarah Phillips, on a miniature merry-go-round bear she made expressly for Carrousel.

Tiny 3½in (9cm) Schuco panda. Hard to find.

A gathering of the clan at the Carrousel Museum.

The Teddy Girl

Rare Teddy Girl with bisque head, 11in (28cm).

Celluloid-faced Teddy Girl, 8½in (22cm).

The bulk of the Carrousel Museum Collection is made up of your basic 18in (46cm) fully-jointed teddy bears with hump back and glass eyes, many of them dating from the 1930s. Sizes and ages vary dramatically from turn-of-the-century up to some pretty unique teddy bears from the 1950s and 1960s. One of the things that makes our collection unique, however, is the broad range of teddy bears and teddy related items. We have had the good fortune of finding some rather rare and unusual items through the years we have been collecting.

Some of the more unique teddies in our collection are the Teddy Girls. These rather unattractive pieces are really half teddy bear and half-doll. They were introduced in 1908 by doll manufacturers who were concerned that, because of the tremendous popularity of the teddy bear, they would not sell many dolls that Christmas. Teddy Girls were, for the most part, a rather crude teddy bear body with a celluloid doll mask for the face, covered with a mohair hood. In spite of their teddy bear connection, sales were dismal and producers were quick to drop them from their line, thus assuring their rarity to today's collector.

Even among the Teddy Girls produced for the market, there were some departures from standard practice. One

manufacturer offered a Teddy Girl with a bisque doll head instead of the celluloid mask face. Our example of this Teddy Girl came to us from a doll collector who purchased a box of miscellaneous parts at an auction and discovered the Teddy Girl with a bisque head inside. Since she felt it was more teddy bear than doll, she was kind enough to let us purchase it for our collection.

We have two examples of the celluloid-faced Teddy Girls in our collection. One has the typical gold mohair body and the other is in an unusual gray color. Most of the Teddy Girls we have seen tend toward the smaller size, usually under 12in (31cm). Our bisque-headed Teddy Girl is 11in (28cm) and our celluloid versions are around 8in (20cm) in size.

One other Teddy Girl has found its way into our collection. This version has a papier-mâché head, an inexpensive material that was also widely used to produce dolls.

While the Teddy Girl lacks the charm and cuddly appeal of the basic teddy bear, a collection that is aimed at including a wide variety of teddy bears and bear related items could include an example or two of this rare teddy bear. Because Teddy Girls lack the appeal of the typical teddy bear, they can sometimes be purchased for a reasonable price, in spite of their rarity.

Teddy Boy with papier-mâché head, 7½in (19cm).

Rare teddy dolls in three mediums.

Come to the Fair

Country fairs and carnivals have offered a variety of premiums and prizes for their games of chance that make up the largest part of the midway. Whether it is a ring toss game or the booth with the milk bottles waiting to be knocked over with a well-thrown baseball, the enticing prizes are usually prominently displayed to draw your attention and get you to open your wallet.

As you review the history of the fairs that have been a part of our heritage over a wide span of years, the prizes that were typically offered had to be eye appealing and inexpensive. Celluloid dolls attached to a cane were common during the 1930s and 1940s, as were plaster statue figures of pets and movie stars or comic characters of the day. Today's carnival is likely to have plastic dolls that have replaced celluloid figures and plaster forms that continue to be popular because they

This carnival teddy is most striking because of his big feet, giving him an almost clown-like appearance, 9½in (24cm).

can be produced at a low cost and still have great eye appeal.

One other premium that was found in most all fairs then as well as now is the teddy bear. When you think about the tremendous appeal of the teddy bear, it is logical that a carnival promoter worth his salt would include a good selection of teddies in his prize line up.

The biggest and best of the prizes, including teddy bears, were found hanging up high so they could be seen from a distance. The bears that were usually awarded were small enough to keep under the counter. They did seem to have one thing in common and that was their untypical color. Bright pinks, reds, greens and other gaudy colors were the rule for carnival bears. Because of this practice, it is easier to recognize an example from a fair or carnival today. That is not to say that all brightly colored bears originated at a carnival or fair, but it is safe to say that most of the prize award teddies at carnivals were brightly colored.

We have a fair variety (pardon the pun) of these interesting teddy bears in our collection. Some of the earlier examples were made in America in the 1930s, and a high percentage of them were produced in Japan and other countries that

1930s 12in (31cm) carnival teddy.

A pair of bears from the fair. Japan. 8in (20cm).

were geared to produce colorful products at a rock-bottom price. Because mohair has always been a relatively expensive fabric to use for teddy bears, it is somewhat unusual to find a carnival prize teddy in mohair. It probably would be an indication that it was made in the 1920s or 1930s.

We have three rather unusual carnival teddies in our collection that are sometimes referred to as soldier bears. We prefer to think that they were made to be Bandsmen Bears. Whatever their original design, they are rather striking examples of a bright teddy bear that has strong eye appeal, but could be manufactured at a low cost. By making the uniform part of the body, the producer could eliminate a great deal of the plush, using it for just the head and tips of the paws. One of our Bandsmen has a simple cardboard tube for his leg, covered with the uniform fabric.

Two of the three Bandsmen Teddies in our collection were made by the same manufacturer, one in a red uniform and the other in a gray outfit. We acquired one of them early in the day at the Antique Toy World Toy Show west of Chicago in St. Charles, Illinois. They hold several shows each year and these shows are one of our favorite sources for antique teddy bears. We obtained the Bandsmen Teddy from a dealer who has just unpacked it; as we were walking out the door to head for another building, a dealer stopped us and asked if we might be interested in "another teddy bear just like that one." It turned out to be exactly like the one we just purchased, different in color only.

We have a third Bandsmen Teddy that was not made by the same manufacturer, but has much of the same appeal and design that our other two have. Their heads are of cotton plush, with glass eyes; they were of American origin, produced some time in the 1920s era.

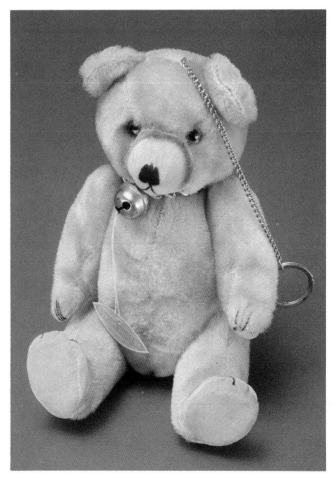

This charming carnival prize came to us complete with original paper label attached to a string. Japan. Circa 1950s. 7½in (19cm).

ABOVE: 1930s Bandsman Bear, 23in (58cm), and a second Bandsman discovered the same day.

RIGHT: A third Bandsman, made by a different company, joins the Carrousel Museum collection. Almost enough to strike up the band!

A fair collection of carnival bears.

Holy Toledo!

Early every summer a unique show takes place in Toledo, Ohio, that draws a specific group of teddy bear collectors from all over the country. It is the annual "Tribute To Steiff" show presented by our friends, Ben and Beth Savino, and their staff from Hobby Center Toys. This is the same organization that puts on one of the largest doll and teddy bear shows in the country, held in Toledo, with "Who's Who" in the doll and teddy bear world on hand to talk to the thousands of collectors who attend.

The Tribute To Steiff is, as the name implies, focused on the world famous Steiff company of Germany, who have been in the forefront of the teddy bear world since its inception. Of all the teddy bears produced, Steiff teddies have certainly commanded the greatest prices for early examples of their work, a tribute to their lasting quality. In addition to the full line of Steiff products offered by Hobby Center Toys, the Savinos have assembled some of the leading antique teddy bear dealers in the country to offer the visiting collectors a variety of antique teddy bears.

Our busy schedule does not always allow us the time to attend the entire Tribute To Steiff program but we always make an effort to take in as much of it as we can, as it is truly an outstanding event, not only for Steiff collectors, but for arctophiles of all interests.

The 1988 Tribute To Steiff show featured an outstanding program presented by Steiff Historian Dr. Jörg Jünginger. A great deal of information not previously known about Steiff was shared with the audience and a lengthy question and answer session followed his presentation. The next day we were on hand when the show opened to check out the offering of antique teddy bears at the booths of the antique dealers from all over the country.

I can state without hesitation that there were many unique and desirable teddy bears to choose from that could easily have been added to our collection but for that one universal problem common among collectors, the limited budget for bears. Since we have to live within our means, I usually want to see every teddy in the show before making my choice or choices but I must also recognize that if I do not buy a particular teddy when I see it, the chances are great that it will be gone when I come back. We have learned that if we find a bear that we really want, we do not set it down until we complete our purchase.

We found such a bear at this show and to add to our "do we or don't we" dilemma, the dealer had not arrived at her booth yet. The bear in question was a blank button Steiff and the price was extremely low. Now, before your heart starts pounding, let me explain that this teddy was in such deplorable condition that many people would debate whether or not to simply discard it or keep it. Our practical side tried to recognize the hours of work needed to bring it into accept-

Restored blank button Steiff, 9½in (24cm), and photograph of bear as found before restoration.

able condition; however, the poor teddy had that "help me, help me" look that simply would not allow you to ignore it and walk away.

Doris scooped up the fragile teddy and held it gently until the dealer came in and she was able to complete the transaction. The mohair had long since been lost to excessive loving, moths or silverfish, and the pawpads had deteriorated to the point where a previous owner simply sewed the ends of the paws closed to keep what little straw stuffing was left intact. In fact, about the only redeeming features remaining were his original ears and eyes and his blank button.

Because of the teddy bear's very fragile fabric, it was difficult to sew without literally pulling the thread right through the material. Doris accepted the challenge and invested the required amount of T.L.C. (tender loving care) to bring poor teddy back to life. Once the repairs were completed, an antique lace collar restored this lady to a measure of dignity befitting a teddy of her age and status.

Why would any reasonable person in their right mind spend money to have the right to spend countless hours working on something that should have been thrown out long ago? Perhaps it is the challenge. Maybe it is a voice inside the teddy that calls to you. Whatever it is, the reward is in seeing the finished work and finding yet another spot on an already crowded shelf.

Two Bit Daniley

Barbara and Bob Lauver are two people that every collector of antique teddy bears should know. They operate a business called Harper General Store in Annville, Pennsylvania, specializing in antique teddy bears. They are typical of most of the teddy bear dealers and collectors we have met over the years, in that they are friendly, sharing and honest. Because prices have escalated so greatly in the past few years, our little hobby has attracted some individuals whose business practices are outright dishonest, or certainly questionable. I am happy to say, however, that by and large most people we have done business with are totally reliable. Barb and Bob could serve as the model for the best in our business.

In addition to selling a great number of antique teddy bears and other children's collectibles at shows, the Lauvers can be found most weekends at the famous Renninger's Antique Market in Pennsylvania, where they have a stall. As an added feature after the Baltimore show every fall, a bus load of teddy collectors are taken north into that wonderful world of antique shops and dealers that abound in Southeastern Pennsylvania. Making just two or three stops with the bus allows us to examine goods offered by literally hundreds of dealers.

We first met Barb and Bob at one Baltimore show several years ago. Since our first love is collecting antique teddy bears, it was only natural that we would discover the Lauvers and their wonderful old teddies. We have purchased several delightful bears from the Lauvers since we first met, but one of our favorites is a beautiful American teddy that has that marvelous expression that we all look for. Barb suggested it was an excellent choice for us because he had a charming story.

She was contacted by a lady who read an article about the Lauvers and their love of teddy bears. The lady was impressed with their candor in stating that old teddy bears were bringing strong prices now so she arranged to meet with them. She showed them the American teddy and told them how she had come to own it. It seems that many years ago she was assisting her church in preparing for a rummage sale and she was assigned to visit some of the parishioners to gather clothing for the sale. She stopped to pick up some items from an elderly gentleman who was taking the goods out of bags. He pulled out the teddy bear and apologizing that she did not want that dirty old bear, tossed it into the corner. "Oh, no," she said, retrieving the bear, "He's a cute teddy. We would love to have him. I will give you a dollar for him." "Too much," said the gentleman, "I want a quarter." After a brief debate, the old man held his ground and the teddy was purchased for twenty-five cents. The lady took the bear home for her little girl.

Time passed and now her daughter was ready for college. The lady had recently read the article about the value of old teddy bears and in sorting out her daughter's possessions, they felt that perhaps some extra money for college might be helpful so the teddy bear made the trip to the Lauvers, where Barb paid many times his original cost to this woman.

His sparkling story, combined with the fact that Doris' grandfather was born and raised in Pennsylvania, prompted us to give him the name of "Two Bit Daniley." He had the honor of attending our first personal appearance at Epcot Center in Florida in the spring of 1988. Since this was his first trip with our traveling collection, we marked the occasion by outfitting him with a red sash, then visiting each of the country exhibits at Epcot Center and buying a country pin to display on his sash.

American teddy bears are now starting to appreciate in value and desirability. This is a typical example of a handsome American teddy.

Ten Dollar Update

Ten dollar teddy bears are few and far between in these days of $10,000.00 teddy bears. We do not have many in our collection but there are a few. If you have only started collecting antique teddy bears within the last few years, chances are good that your collection does not include many of the $10.00 variety. However, if your bear addiction goes back ten years or more, you may well have several old bears that were acquired for $10.00 and even less. When we started collecting in the mid 1970s, you did not admit in public that you collected teddy bears. At that time we were specializing in selling antique toys and dolls and there was rarely a call for a teddy bear. When you did find one, it was more likely to be in a dealer's box under his table rather than on display on his shelves.

Good examples of early German teddies in mint condition might fetch as much as $200.00 but the average run-of-the-mill slightly worn teddy from the 1930s could be purchased for $25.00, plus or minus a fin. If you were a real shopper and asked if the shop you were visiting had any old teddy bears, you would sometimes get a favorable response and the shop owner would retreat to the back room to bring out a teddy bear.

Such was the case at a small shop adjacent to the owner's house in Indiana some years ago. After carefully checking

Well loved (and worn) 1930s Schuco compact teddy.

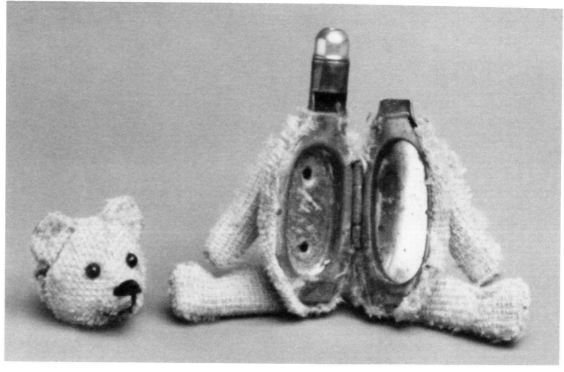

3in (8cm) compact in open position.

the entire shop for toys and dolls, we informed the owner of our teddy bear collection and how we were also looking for unusual examples to add to our family. We talked in particular about some of the rare pieces and specifically mentioned a rare Schuco perfume teddy. "There was a companion piece to this bear that was a little teddy with a compact hidden inside," I concluded, "and some day we hope to find that one." "I believe I had one as a child," the owner responded. "Have you got a minute?"

"Lady, I've got all day." I replied, and with that, she suggested we watch the shop as she went next door to her home. She was back in about 15 minutes clutching the tiny Schuco compact bear. All that was left of his covering was the pink backing of the mohair. Since this bear was in such poor condition, she decided she was willing to part with it for $10.00. Even in that condition, even in the mid 1970s, this rare teddy was well worth her asking price.

We have shared this story on many of our personal appearances and it was included in our first book. However, the update needs to be shared now. It happened in 1987 in Memphis, Tennessee, during one of our shop appearances. We were at a marvelous toy store called Childhood Trea-

This Schuco compact bear is in mint condition.

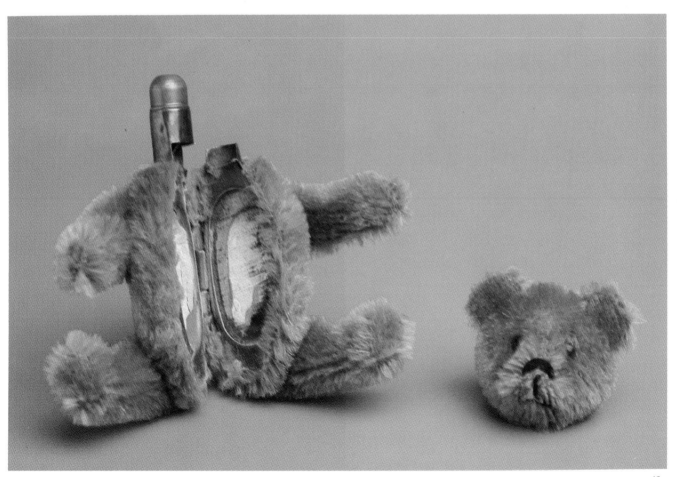

sures. A local antique dealer came in to see us and brought along a Schuco compact teddy to share with us. It was an unusual purple color and it had been originally purchased from a gift shop in the famous Peabody Hotel. This is the hotel where a daily parade of ducks make their way through the lobby, which has given the place world-wide publicity over the years.

The antique dealer suggested that there were not any teddy bear collectors in the area and when I asked why she felt that way, she said, "because nobody wants to pay what I think this bear is worth." I asked what she felt it was worth and she said, "$300.00." "You just sold it," I responded, reaching for my checkbook. It was obviously a good buy at that price and I think I was still feeling a little guilty over my well-worn find ten years previous that was priced at $10.00.

When Is a Teddy Not a Teddy

The Carrousel Museum Collection is made up by and large of the traditional plush, jointed, glass-eyed teddy bears. However, we are occasionally drawn to teddy bears that are made of some other media, be it glass, porcelain, tin or some other material. We feel it adds interest to the collection and gives it a flavor that enhances, rather than detracts from the basic bears.

One of the more interesting and rare items in this category was acquired at a large monthly antique market in Ann Arbor, Michigan. The show attracts dealers from several states and there are usually a number of teddy bears among the offerings. Two years ago we attended the market and discovered what can best be described as a jack-in-the-box teddy bear. It is a plush teddy in that it has the typical head and arms, but that it departs from tradition in that the body appears to be a tapered skirt going to the base, which is closed off across the bottom. The real surprise comes when you discover that the body contains a spring, allowing you to compress the head toward the base in a jack-in-the-box fashion. That is probably not the best term, since we doubt that this teddy was ever enclosed in a box, due to the mohair fabric on the body being the same color as the head. If it had been in a box, there would be some fading of the head fabric. We have only seen one other like this bear; it was offered at Linda Mullins' San Diego show in January of 1989.

Another piece that is certainly hard to find, if not rare, is a bottle warmer teddy. This bear has a zippered front that allows you to open him up and place the baby's bottle inside to keep it warm. Our example is from the 1940s and we have seen later versions as well.

A teddy bear muff is not considered unusual but it certainly departs from being a basic bear. Since they were used by little girls to keep their hands warm in cold climates, they are more often found in northern states. We have a teddy muff that dates from the 1920s and is in excellent condition.

In Britain we were able to acquire an unusual candy container teddy bear that is made with a tin container inside. Access is gained by removing the head, which is held onto the metal lid with a magnet. The container is well marked on the bottom and is of German origin. A lady who grew up in Germany said there were other animals in this style and it was common to find one under the Christmas tree.

Our son, Jim, found the hot water bottle teddy bear for us just a few years ago. It is a unique example of a modern teddy that is not a teddy. Celluloid teddy bears came on the market around the same time as celluloid dolls appeared in the late teens or early twenties. We have a celluloid bear in a boot that squeaks when the head is pressed down and a celluloid teddy that contains a cloth tape measure.

A teddy bear that originated in England is made of terracotta and is outfitted as a soccer player. It was a welcome gift

A rare jack-in-the-box-style teddy, circa 1920, 9½in (24cm).

A large internal spring allows the jack-in-the-box teddy to be collapsed.

10in (25cm) bottle warmer teddy bear.

The zippered front opens to reveal baby's bottle.

that we received when we first started collecting. Another treasure acquired more recently is a tiny lead soldier teddy bear that was made in France and purchased on our last visit to England.

There seems to be no end to the ingenuity displayed by teddy bear makers and producers in the old days as well as now, and it adds a pleasant flavor to searching for teddy bears and discovering a bear in a previously unknown form.

Hard-to-find teddy bear muff, circa 1920s.

Unusual teddy bear candy container.

This teddy bear hot water bottle will really keep you warm in bed.

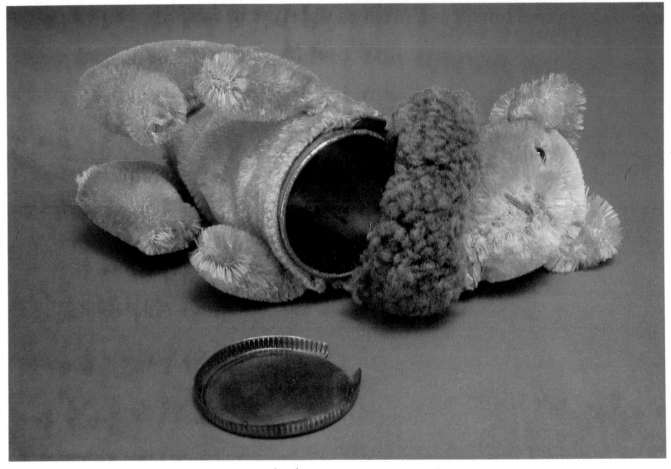

Magnetic head removes to open tin container.

Teddy bear in a boot. Celluloid construction.

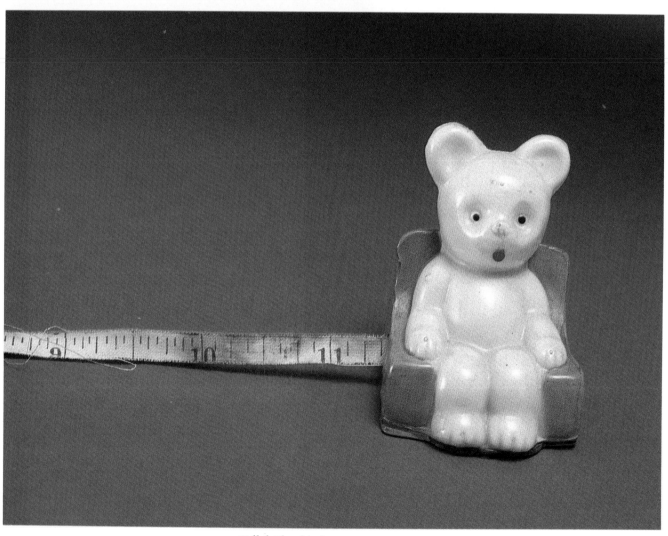

Celluloid teddy bear tape measure.

2½in (6cm) terra-cotta bear from England.

Miniature 1⅜in (4cm) lead soldier teddy made in France.

The Colonel

Chicago, Illinois, is home to an upscale toy store called "Saturday's Child." This beautiful shop is owned and operated by Marcia Nordine, who firmly believes in providing quality merchandise to the many young, married people who are moving into the newly renovated area not far from downtown. This whole section of Halstead Street has turned into a charming shopping district.

We have made several personal appearances at Marcia's lovely store, usually tied in with her shop's anniversary in October. One of the unusual promotions put on by the quaint stores here is called Midnight Madness and all the stores are open until midnight for this event. It made for a rather long day for us, but our tired feelings were more than offset by the many collectors who came by to see our traveling collection of antique teddy bears and to purchase our handcrafted teddies.

Our first appearance at Saturday's Child was in 1983 and we were interviewed at the store by the *Chicago Tribune*. The article appeared in the following Sunday's edition and talked at length about our traveling collection and some of the rare pieces being shown. Several weeks later we received a letter from a lady in Louisville, Kentucky. Her sister had sent her a copy of the article and since she was just closing out her mother's estate, she wanted to get an appraisal on three bears from the remaining belongings.

Enclosed were photographs of the bears. One was a polar bear, a second was a rather nondescript teddy and the third was a splendid white Steiff, all from the 1905 to 1910 era. It is difficult enough to do identification on teddy bears when you have the opportunity to carefully examine them but it is almost impossible to do an adequate job from a photograph. We never recommend that a teddy be shipped by mail because there is always a risk of having it lost so we do the best we can under the circumstances.

We returned the photographs to the lady, along with an estimate of current value. We also recommended that she take the bears to a minimum of two other antique dealers to get a cross section of estimated values so she could be comfortable with the prices given. With our response, we suggested that if she did decide to sell the bears, we were interested in the white Steiff.

A month or so passed and we got a call from the lady saying she was willing to sell the Steiff bear to us. She had obtained prices from three additional antique dealers and felt that our estimate was the best. Once the bear arrived, further examination revealed a bad split in the mohair on the right leg. This is something that would not show up in a photograph so it supports our statement that it is not possible to do a complete evaluation from a picture.

In spite of teddy's frail condition, he was much too admirable to even consider returning so he remains in our collection. Since he came from Louisville, we felt it appropriate to call him "The Colonel." I suspect he likes bourbon as well.

Early Steiff 16in (41cm) from original owner in Louisville, Kentucky.

The Toy Maker

We collect teddy bears, we make bears, we speak and write about bears, we spend all of our waking hours (and some of our sleeping hours) involved with teddy bears. When we reach the saturation point, which happens about once every two years or so, we make a pact to get away for a few days with no teddy bear involvement of any kind. This means no stopping at antique shops or shows, no bear making or designing; in fact, we agree to not even discuss teddy bears. That is similar to telling an ice cream cone not to melt, but at least we have good intentions.

One of our "no bear" weekends happened several years ago and came about as a last minute decision. I had been traveling a good deal in my former job and we had just completed a large Special Edition order for a client. We were reaching the point where teddy bears were starting to become a chore instead of a pleasure so it was time to get away. We did not have a shop to worry about then so we put away the sewing machine and headed north with only a vague goal of getting to the Traverse City area.

By dark we reached our destination and settled into a

21in (53cm) German teddy bear, circa 1910.

49

comfortable motel after an evening meal. A few hours of television added to the weariness of the day's driving so we called it a night.

The next morning we decided to explore the area and headed first for the Sleeping Bear sand dunes just a short drive from Traverse City. It was a pleasant day to visit the dunes and after climbing the big sand hill and walking along the shore, we dumped the excess sand out of our shoes and started down the road. It did not register at the time that the sand dunes were called Sleeping Bear so our vow was already broken.

We headed north on Highway 31, a beautiful drive that runs along Lake Michigan, planning to explore the Charlevoix area, one of Michigan's top tourist attractions. There

are many antique shops in the area but we had managed to avoid them so far, so we planned to spend some time on the beach and along the shore just relaxing. Doris and I both grew up in Alpena, Michigan, on Lake Huron, so we have always had a fondness for any area along the Great Lakes' shoreline.

Lunch time found us passing through the village of Eastport at the tip of Torch Lake. We passed by a small shop with a sign that stated "Restaurant and Bakery" and opted to circle the block and stop. You had to pass right by a showcase filled with cookies, cakes and other delights to get to the half dozen tables at the back of the room. A neatly typed menu was placed before us and the waitress said she would be right back after giving us a small town friendly greeting.

We scanned the menu to find something that would go good with homemade pie and were absorbed in thoughts of making our choice when the waitress returned to our table. "Are you teddy bear lovers?" she asked. We stared at each other in amazement, thinking our friend was clairvoyant. "The purse," she exclaimed, "The cute little teddy bear in your purse, ma'am." With that, we both chuckled aloud and admitted to our addiction.

After a brief discussion about our collection, we got back to the business at hand and ordered a light sandwich so it would not interfere with dessert. When our new friend returned with our check, she said that she had an old teddy bear at home that was brought to this country by her mother, a German immigrant. This lady was on the plus side of 50, so we made a quick mental estimate of a teddy from the early 1900s. Since she had no one to leave it to, she suggested that she would be willing to sell it.

We agreed to return at 4 o'clock when she got off work to follow her home to see the bear. After all, she brought up the subject of teddy bears so it was OK to check out this one teddy, right? We spent a very long three hours or so beachcombing in the area, returning to the restaurant a few minutes before our appointed time. Since it was a small community, it did not take long to reach her pleasant home just a few blocks away. Teddy was sitting in a living room chair as we entered and it was love at first sight. Our enthusiasm was heightened when we learned that the owner's grandfather was a toy maker in Nüremberg, Germany. It brought forth visions of many of the early German tin toys that had passed through our hands over the past few years as antique dealers.

The felt top hat and velvet cape were added to the bear some time during his lifetime, adding to his warm appearance. I cannot tell you what we did for the rest of the weekend but it will long be remembered as the best "non-bear" weekend we ever had.

Teddy in formal dress, ready for a night at the opera.

Teddy plays with a German tin toy that is older than he is!

No Wear On This Bear Nowhere

24in (61cm) early American teddy in pristine condition.

Teddy bears and dolls have always been a great combination for many collectors. We find a lot of bear collectors who occasionally add a doll or two to their collection and the same is true of doll collectors. Since doll collecting is an even bigger hobby than ours, it makes sense that if you are looking for old teddy bears, chances are good of finding some at a doll show and sale. In fact, when we started collecting, there were no teddy bear shows as such; doll shows and antique shows were the primary hunting grounds.

In Saginaw, Michigan, the area doll club sponsors an annual show at the Civic Center that brings together all phases of the doll world, from antique to modern to hand-crafted, much as some of our teddy bear shows do. We make a special effort to attend this show because we know many of the dealers who set up there, having dealt in toys and dolls for many years.

Our usual pattern in shopping a show is to get there early and once the show opens, pass through quickly, scanning all the booths as we go. If we see that special face or unique teddy bear on a table, we stop to check it out. Once we have made the rounds of the entire show, we then go back and start over, taking our time to examine everything carefully. With two of us shopping, we can cover more area in a faster time, being careful not to get out of sight of each other so we can stop to check out a special teddy.

Since this show only takes place once a year, it draws large crowds, making it difficult to move through the narrow aisles. The crowds thin out by mid afternoon but by then, most of the better bears have found new homes, so it is best to be early and be patient.

As we made our way through the show in 1984, I glanced across to the next aisle, where I saw a very large teddy bear sitting on the top shelf of a dealer's table. I did not give it a great deal of attention as it appeared to be a new teddy because of its pristine condition and my interest at the moment was antique bears. When we finally made our second pass through the show, I stopped to examine the bear more closely and was thrilled to discover that it was, in fact, an early American teddy, perhaps an Ideal, in mint condition. The dealer said that the owner had it carefully wrapped in tissue paper and put away in a bureau drawer. Finding teddy bears in this condition always fills us with mixed emotions. We are pleased to find the rare unplayed with bear, but you always wonder why it is not played with and you cannot help but feel that perhaps the child never had the opportunity to love it.

When we examined the price tag, we discovered why this teddy had not been snapped up by another collector before we got to it. The price was higher than we had ever paid for a teddy bear at that point in time and so reluctantly, we returned him to the shelf.

During the ensuing several weeks, we frequently thought about the big bear. We finally sat down and rationalized that a mint condition teddy of this size and age (24in [61cm] circa 1915) only comes along once in a lifetime and we might never get another opportunity to buy one like him. We frantically searched our files for the antique dealer's name and called. We held our breath until we found out that she still had the bear. A check was mailed that day and within a week or so this absolutely marvelous teddy joined our family.

It is true. We did have to go on a hotdog diet for awhile and forego movies and other nonessentials, but as usual, you somehow manage to make ends meet and add that special teddy to your collection. As a rule, we try to follow the practice of buying the bear we want when we see it because it is almost always gone when you go back. Thank goodness this was the exception to the rule.

Miniature Teddy Bears — Then and Now

Doris and I have a special fondness in our hearts for miniature teddy bears and the artists who create them. One of the reasons we like them is probably related to the fact that we do not make them. We know what goes into making the full-size teddies so we are in awe of those who can create the same detailed features in miniature. Generally speaking, miniature bears are those from perhaps about 4in (10cm) in size and smaller. There is no hard and fast rule regarding that and I would agree that 5 and 6in (13 and 15cm) teddy bears are certainly small but as a rule we are speaking of 4in (10cm) and smaller when we speak of miniature teddy bears.

Because of their tiny size, it is easy to overlook miniature teddy bears when you are shopping at an antique shop or show. Make a point of checking out those flat top jewelry cases dealers generally have on their counters, for that is where the little bears like to hide. We have several old miniature teddies in our collection, unidentified as to maker or country of origin, but welcome additions none the less. One 3in (8cm) jointed teddy that was previously believed to be of Japanese origin is actually from East Germany. Our example still has the identifying paper label on one foot. Since it was a stick-on paper label, it probably got pulled off or fell off most of the time.

4¼in (11cm) miniature teddy, circa 1920s.

3½in (9cm) tiny teddy bear from 1930s era.

Unusual teddy from East Germany. Note paper label on foot.

Another that we consider a miniature even though it actually measures 6½in (17cm) has a handmade flapper outfit. The head ribbon had to be replaced as it was literally falling away in pieces. This teddy even looks like a flapper!

Old examples of miniature teddy bears are especially difficult to find so we have expanded our collection with tiny bears by contemporary artists.

One outstanding miniature artist that is represented in our collection is a charming lady named Dickie Harrison of Baltimore. Dickie's daughter, Donna, has been involved in the Baltimore show and convention for a number of years and it was through Donna that we became acquainted with her mother's detailed teddies. Dickie was first a miniaturist and because of her daughter's teddy bear collecting, Dickie started with miniature bears.

Two delightful miniaturists who are frequently sharing a table at shows are Elaine Fujita Gamble and Lori Sasaki. Their tiny teddies are so sought after at shows that if you are not there when they set up, chances are their bears will be gone within a half hour or so. We make it a point to get in line early, as their work is excellent.

Linda Kuhn is a talented miniaturist from the Cleveland, Ohio, area. We met her and her daughter, Kathy Thomas, (who makes the delightful Golliwoggs we mentioned in an earlier chapter) at the Baltimore Show and Convention in 1988. Once you pick up one of Linda's tiny teddy bears, you know it is going home with you. Her expressions are just priceless.

As we stated earlier, we do not make miniature teddy bears ourselves so we have great respect for those who do. Another miniature teddy maker turned up a little closer to home recently. All three of our daughters have been involved in our business to one degree or another. Kim, our youngest, spent several years teaching in California so she did not have the opportunity to participate as much as we would like because she does great work when she is available. She is currently back in college to get her master's degree so we again have the opportunity to put her to work. Patty Messinger, our middle daughter, works full time for us and manages our shop when we are on the road, which is frequently. We would not be able to carry on our business without her able assistance. Our oldest girl, Mary Baese, is a full-time dental hygienist and spends a limited amount of time making Carrousel Teddy Bears. We were surprised and thrilled to find that she has a talent for making miniature teddies.

Mary announced a short time ago that she would like to try her hand at making them and did her first from a kit. The result was so pleasing that she has continued with her own designs. Maybe you will soon see a series of Carrousel by Michaud teddies in miniature size, only the label will have to read, "Carrousel by Baese."

One of our favorite antique miniature teddies dressed in her flapper outfit, 6½in (16cm).

4in (10cm) charmer by Elaine Fujita Gamble.

54

Dickie Harrison created this 3in (8cm) teddy.

2¼in (6cm) teddy bear by California Artist Lori Sasaki.

This tiny teddy by Artist Linda Kuhn will capture your heart.

Does this little teddy resemble a Carrousel by Michaud Bear? It was one of the first miniature teddies created by our daughter, Mary Baese, a new talent on the miniature scene.

Great things do come in small packages.

Mechanical Bears

11in (28cm) weight lifter from the 1950s. Japan.

It is probably my engineering background but I have always had a fascination for mechanical toys, including teddy bears. These delightful animated playthings go back probably as far as toys themselves. Just as soon as a toy was produced, some engineering type sat down and figured out how to make it roll, fly, spin or do something unusual.

French automatons are particularly sought after by toy and doll collectors all over the world and they command the highest prices when they are offered at auction. The Germans were also very adept at the art of building mechanical toys. Schuco was a German firm that specialized in a wide variety of mechanical toys, including teddy bears. We have several prized Schuco bears in our collection, including their yes/no teddy bear that responded to the movement of his tail. We also have the hard-to-find Schuco tumbling bear that performs somersaults with the turn of his key, and a delightful little bear that has a vibrating mechanism within his body that causes him to dance around a tabletop.

If I were giving an award for sheer genius in creating complicated mechanical movements in toys and maintaining a low market price, it would have to go to the Japanese toy makers. Our collection includes some of the earlier 1920s and 1930s toys made in Japan, and referred to by toy collectors as "Paper Label Japan" because they almost always had a small paper label stating the country of origin. Since it was simply a stick-on label, it more often than not fell off or was removed.

The real heyday of the Japanese mechanical toy manufacturer was in the 1950s, with a huge array of clever performing toys flooding our market. They were very inexpensive and produced in large numbers. Unfortunately, we were not blessed with hindsight when we were dealing in antique toys and passed up literally hundreds of these unique toys, feeling that they would never be collectible due to their large production numbers. How wrong we were! Mechanical toys from the 1950s that we passed up for $5.00 to $10.00 are now commanding prices of $100.00 for the common examples, with some hard-to-find robots selling for over $1000.00. I was told many years ago by an experienced antique dealer that the secret to success was to watch for the sleepers. Buy the items that are plentiful and reasonably priced now, that will rapidly rise in price in ten years. Good advice, but difficult to predict.

There was no shortage of performing bears among the 1950s Japanese toys and some are absolutely ingenious. We

This cola-drinking panda is eagerly sought by beverage collectors as well as arctophiles. 11in (28cm).

8½in (22cm) mechanical teddy sits up when alarm rings. Japan. Circa 1950s.

Momma bear takes her baby for a stroll. Windup from Japan.

have a teddy that lies sleeping in a bed and when the alarm at the head of the bed goes off, teddy sits up, stretches and yawns, letting out a squeal, then lays back down for a few more winks. How realistic can you get? Another popular mechanical toy is the bear that pours milk from a bottle into a glass, then takes a drink and repeats the action. This same company made the same bear holding a cola bottle, but it is equally sought by cola collectors, so it is usually priced higher.

Today's manufacturers have not overlooked the popularity of mechanical teddy bears and a visit to most any toy or teddy shop will be rewarded with a good selection. One of the most popular teddies last year was a roller skating teddy bear that also played a tune to skate to. It was the microchip music that is so popular in modern toys and the bear skated along, keeping perfect time to the music. This unique toy was in demand by bear collectors, music box collectors, toy collectors and people who did not collect anything but were simply fascinated with its creative performance.

We discovered a new mechanical toy this past year that took over the popularity of the skating teddy. It was a walking, growling bear that took a half dozen steps or so, stopped and growled as his head rolled from side to side and his mouth opened. His popularity was unfortunately over-

5in (13cm) Schuco dancing teddy bear.

shadowed by a companion mechanical toy made by the same company. It was a pig that took several steps, stopped and oinked, complete with vibrating snout and tail, then continued his walk.

You may have to shop around a little, but these and other totally captivating mechanical bears and toys are still on the market. At their low price, it is worth speculating a little and buying them for future investment. At least that is my argument when I walk out the door with my purchase.

Somersaulting Schuco mechanical teddy, 4in (10cm).

Mechanical wooden bear made in Russia.

Beauty Is in the Eye of the Beholder

Teddy bears are like children. There are no two alike. We have been making this claim for years now and it is true. Even with the same person producing the features on the bear, they just do not turn out to be twins. We view this as a plus because the teddy's character is expressed in his facial appearance. Sometimes an exaggerated body shape adds to the outlandish look of a particular bear but basically, the major portion of his or her character is developed by the facial expression.

Doris has a tendency to want each of our handcrafted teddies to be perfect, but sometimes a little imperfection is desirable in developing an eccentric look. Character teddies are sometimes planned that way and sometimes it is coincidental. One of our most popular character bears is one we call "Just Ted." He was given to his original owner in 1924 and he has a right ear that is lower on the head than the left, giving him a lopsided, lovable appearance. We believed for many years that the person who sewed his ears on slipped a little but we have recently received a letter from a lady who saw his picture in a magazine and wrote to tell us it is exactly like her mother's cherished teddy bear.

It is amazing how a minor change in the teddy bear's features can make a major change in his character. If you are a bear maker, take one of your basic bears and simply make his ears half again as big as you normally make them. Or, make them the same size, but sew them on lower on the head and tilted forward at a slight angle. You can also give your bear a totally different look by moving his eyes up or down just a fraction of an inch.

Sometimes the teddy's character suggests a name for him. This was the case with a rather rotund British bear we acquired at a show several years ago. In examining him, we turned him sideways to see his profile and the name "Alfred" popped out. His profile was a perfect likeness of the late mystery writer, Alfred Hitchcock. On more than one occasion we have walked away from a show with a teddy bear that was purchased, not on the basis of who made him, how old he was or how he was priced, but solely because he had that look that said, "Take me home."

Teddy bears can look mad, sad or glad. They can be passive, pensive or positive. They can be hungry, homesick or happy. In fact, there is one sitting across the table from me with that excited look that says, "Hey, tell them about me!" He will just have to be patient and wait for another chapter.

20in (51cm) teddy. Maker unknown. Circa 1930s.

Is it time to get up already?

24in (61cm) American teddy bear from the 1920s.

American 20in (51cm) teddy from 1930s.

"Oh please, oh please, oh please take me home!"

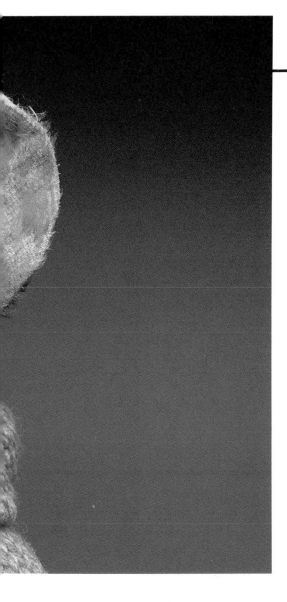

19in (48cm) British teddy with tin eyes. 1930s.

"No, I'm not related to Marty Feldman."

British 18in (46cm) bear from the 1920s.

"They say I look like Alfred Hitchcock. Preposterous!"

Berliner Bear, made in many sizes and styles over the years. This example has a composition face.

"Pass the Wienerschnitzel, please."

A Photo Essay

The Carrousel Museum Collection is concentrated on antique jointed, mohair teddy bears, but by no means limited to our fuzzy friends. We have a number of items that fall into the category of bearaphernalia (see Chapter 25) and add interest to any collection. Items that would fit into this category are photographs and post cards of children with teddy bears. Our experience shows that these interesting photographs are almost as hard to find as teddy bears themselves!

When they are discovered, they can usually be purchased for just a few dollars, although we have seen them offered by some post card dealers for up to $10.00 each. In the early days before cameras became a common household article, roving photographers made a living by going from house to house, taking photographs of the children. It was common practice to have them pose with a pet, or perhaps a favorite doll or teddy bear. We have a photograph in our family showing me along with my twin sister photographed on a pony in our back yard. The finished photograph is actually on post card stock.

A number of widely recognized teddy bear collections have photographs and post cards included. Paul and Rose-

Remembrance

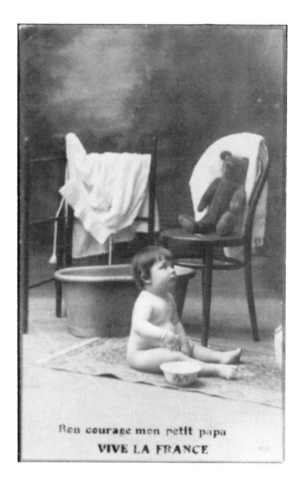

Bon courage mon petit papa
VIVE LA FRANCE

mary Volpp of California have one of the world's most outstanding teddy bear collections and Paul has a large number of teddy bear post cards that were commercially produced in the 1920s and 1930s. The Cracker Jack Company did a series of Teddy B. and Teddy G. cards that came individually in boxes of Cracker Jacks, or you could send for the entire set of 16 cards. There were many other commercially produced cards as well and it can be a challenge to complete a series.

Joan Venturino, one of the pioneer teddy bear store owners from California, collects the actual photographs of children and teddies, and she has been able to obtain enough background information on many of the families to do a marvelous presentation at teddy bear shows and conventions. Even when you are not able to get the real story behind the picture, it is great fun to speculate on what the story might be.

We present herewith a selection of some of the more interesting photographs from our collection for you to ponder.

Doris Duquesne.

Bill Boyd's Beautiful Bears

Mr. Billian, an all original Germany teddy, circa 1930. 12½in (32cm).

Bill Boyd is a fellow bear collector from Kansas, and although we have not had the pleasure of seeing his collection, we have been told by several people that it is truly outstanding. When we first met Bill a few years ago, he told us he had been collecting for some 20 years. He has a background as an antique dealer so we have a number of

things in common. Bill has had several teddies come his way under unusual circumstances.

He told us of a teddy tour he took to Europe in 1987, visiting six teddy bear factories, antique shops and flea markets. In Bamberg, West Germany, the local newspaper did an article about the Americans who were in town looking for old teddies. The article suggested that residents who had bears to sell could take them to the hotel. The group drew lots to purchase any bears brought to the hotel but Bill's number never came up.

At the end of the day a woman called the hotel to say she had two bears to sell but could not come to the hotel. The message was eventually passed on to Bill and his roommate, with just an address. After getting lost and getting directions from a nanny with a baby, they found the apartment house and on the fifth try, they got the right apartment. Bill's friend had limited skills with his German but they were able to communicate through a few words and sign language. The lady produced two teddies in a plastic bag and insisted they take them. Bill and his friend insisted on paying for them but she would not hear of it. On their return to the hotel, they decided who would get which bear; Bill named his "Mr. Billian," after the lady's husband. The teddies date from the 1920s and 1930s and Bill has continued to correspond with his wonderful German friend. Mr. Billian is a fully-jointed 12½in (32cm) teddy and his clothing is all original.

Another marvelous teddy bear came to Bill's collection as a result of an article in *Missouri Life Magazine* in 1981. Bill was contacted by a lady who received a delightful teddy in 1906 from her father. She was very fond of her teddy but she recalled that as a child, she would occasionally become angry and hit her teddy on the nose, asking him to explain why this or that happened. He took her punches with loving understanding and never complained. In addition to acquiring this beautiful teddy bear, Bill was also able to acquire a photograph of the original owner as a child with her teddy bear. The lady has since passed on and Bill named the bear "Dicky," which was the owner's last name. Dicky is 19in (48cm) tall, in a tan gold mohair. He has black clear glass eyes and his pads are a peach color tan felt. His sewn nose and claws are a reddish brown thread. Dicky is the senior bear in Bill's collection and has won several awards in teddy contests.

It looks like Doris and I are just going to have to make a trip to see the Boyd collection some day. I have a feeling there are some other charming stories there as well.

Dicky is a 1906 teddy, shown with a photograph of his original owner.

Bearaphernalia

Teddy Carrousel ornament by Hallmark for baby's first Christmas.

German china pitcher from child's set, 3½in (9cm).

If it is not fuzzy, jointed, cuddly or otherwise resembling the classic teddy bear, but has something to do with teddy bears, it could probably fit into the category of bearaphernalia. As we pointed out earlier, it can add a new dimension to a collection of teddy bears to add some of the related items that were produced over the years.

The appeal of the teddy bear was capitalized on by manufacturers who felt the sale of their product could be enhanced by putting a cute teddy bear on it. We have several pieces of children's dish sets in the teddy motif. A cup and saucer showing teddies in various sports activities including soccer date from the 1930s. The fact that one bear is engaged in soccer would lead us to believe that the children's ware was probably sold in England.

One of the more unusual pieces of children's ware we have is a complete set of silverware in a box we purchased from a local antique dealer about ten years ago. Each piece in this set has a bear imprinted on the handle. It would be fun to set up a display of teddy bears at a tea party, using dishes and silverware with teddies on them.

Political memorabilia offers a number of opportunities to add teddy bear related items to your collection. Theodore Roosevelt was so identified with the teddy bear that it became an important part of his political campaigns, appearing in posters, advertisements and political pins. One such pin that has thus far managed to escape our collection is a rare tiny teddy that was actually attached to a ribbon, with a pin of Theodore Roosevelt at the top. Since it is also sought by political collectors, it is particularly hard to find. We do have a campaign pin of painted tin that shows a cartoon version of President Roosevelt as a teddy bear.

Puzzles were frequently themed on teddy bears; one small novelty in our collection was probably given as a premium at a carnival or fair. It is a tiny container with a glass top that shows a printed teddy inside. There is a tiny metal knife and fork, and the objective is to jiggle the puzzle around until the silverware comes to rest in his paws.

Advertising is another good source for teddy bears or bears in general, including grape box labels. We have found several bears printed on these collectable art forms. Old magazines can also be a source for various advertisements focused on teddy bears. We found a charming advertisement showing the Dionne Quintuplets, each holding a teddy bear. It was an ad for Palmolive soap. I cannot say for certain that the Quints had a teddy bear but it would be hard to believe that with all of the gifts that were showered on these world famous children, that there were not a number of teddy bears included.

Just as you could fill a large book with examples of the variety of teddy bears that were produced, you could fill a companion book with bearaphernalia through the years, and probably not even scratch the surface of the unlimited things that included the teddy bear in one form or another.

Child's tea set in teddy motif from Germany.

Porcelain figure of girl with red teddy bear.

Unusual porcelain pincushion teddy.

Limited edition Teddy Roosevelt figure produced by well-known arctophile, Bill Boyd, from the Kansas City area.

Silver bookmark with advertising on back.

Tiny box puzzle that tests your skill in shaking the box until silverware is caught in teddy's paws!

Early mechanical teddy reprinted in puzzle form.

Grape box bear label.

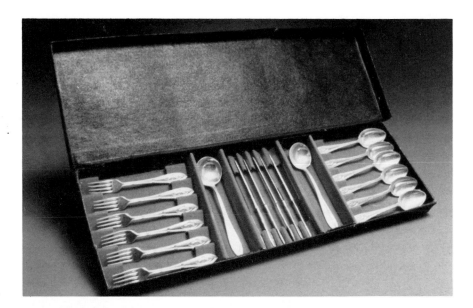

Complete set of child's silverware.

*Each piece of silverware has a bear em-
bossed on the handle.*

This Teddy Is a Lady

Second Hand Rose (left) attired in her second hand clothes, American, circa 1915, 15in (38cm), with Carrousel recreation.

When you read stories about teddy bears or see a description in an advertisement, they are invariably referred to as "He," "Him," or some other expression in the male gender. It is true, most teddies are boy bears, probably due in large part to their macho namesake, Theodore Roosevelt. This was one of the most rugged, manly Presidents we have ever had. He was an outdoorsman, a sportsman, hunter and Rough Rider. President Roosevelt was so closely associated with the teddy bear that it became an important part of his campaigns.

Does that mean, then, that all teddy bears are masculine? Absolutely not! Some teddies were created by their designer to be female, while others have that certain look that tells you that this bear calls for a lace collar, a feathered hat or some other type of female adornment. We purchased one lady bear at a show in San Jose, California, simply because it was a she. Her dress was part of the body so there was no

18in (46cm). American teddy.

This charming lady is from the 1920s, 14in (36cm).

A most unusual lady teddy with a metal nose. Circa 1930s.

question what the creator had in mind. As it turned out, she was part of a three-bear set of Mama, Papa and Baby. Some years later we found Baby but we have never been able to locate Papa. If you see him, tell him to call Home!

Some antique dealer friends of ours found a wonderful teddy bear in a steamer trunk in the attic of an old estate they purchased. It was not dressed in costume but since our dealer friends specialize in period costumes, we opted to dress the bear in an old fur neck piece, a flowered hat and a purse on a shoulder chain. We shared her at a number of shows around the United States before her name turned up. An admirer in Texas, hearing her story, suggested that she should be called Second Hand Rose, and she has been called by that name since. She was our 1989 Museum Recreation in our line of handcrafted teddies and has turned out to be one of the most popular in the line.

Another teddy bear we acquired adopted an early felt hat that came from a box of doll supplies and it was apparent that she was destined to be a lady bear. She is fondly referred to as "Aunt Fanny," with no resemblance to any relatives on either side of our families. She is an 18in (46cm) teddy of American origin, and has an appropriate haughty appearance with her hat in place.

A smaller but equally as charming teddy lady in our group has managed to come up with a genuine Shirley Temple pink felt hat from the 1930s. When we dealt in antique toys and dolls, we were always picking up odd bits and pieces at shows to put away in a goody box for future use. Our teddy bears have managed to deplete several goody boxes in search of appropriate attire.

For some reason, British teddy bears from the 1930s and 1940s seem to adapt well to being dressed as ladies. Perhaps it is the typical broad face found on bears from England that gives them some of the soft and gentle qualities needed in female teddy bears. Several of the many teddy bears that have made the return trip from Great Britain to our home have ended up with a little ribbon in the hair or an outfit of lace.

Some of today's teddy bear artists are particularly good at bringing out female qualities in their bears. Some do them in very elaborate costuming, and still others present their girl bears more in an obvious body form than fancy dress. This is especially evident in Ted Menten's fascinating satirical book titled *Teddy Bearzar*. Ted enlisted the help of a dozen or more top teddy artists and created some magnificent teddy ladies to parody some of the top designer fashions and products that are seen in the high fashion scene. Ted and his talented friends have managed to present some female bears that have never been seen before. It is a fun book that belongs in every bear lover's collection.

Doris and I do not always dress a teddy bear when it comes into our collection and we usually prefer rather simple adornment when we do, such as a lace collar, or maybe just a hat, or something simple. But it is surprising how just a light touch of some odd piece of costuming can bring out a marvelous character. Pick out a rather plain teddy from your collection and search throught the house to find some odd bit of wearing apparel, or maybe even an old pair of glasses. You may be surprised and delighted with the results.

American teddy bear, 14in (36cm).

The girls' night out.

Sound Off

First issue Smokey Bear. 1950s. 15in (38cm).

This teddy speaks fluent German. 20in (51cm). Early 1950s.

"If only teddy bears could talk, think of the wonderful stories they could tell." is a phrase we have heard many times. The fact is, some teddy bears can and do talk. Sometimes you have to do a bit of interpreting, but most arctophiles are rather good at understanding what their teddy bear is saying to them.

We have a teddy that came to us from a couple who said their son was in occupied Germany right after World War II and he purchased it there. This fascinating teddy speaks a number of phrases when you pull the cord at his side but the phrases are all in German. His voice box tends to be somewhat tempermental so it is difficult for even someone fluent in German to catch every word but with the kind assistance of our good friend, Peter Kalinke, the Hermann representative in the United States, we learned that our teddy talks in words of love. It is a quality bear in mohair and was probably rather expensive when it was new in the early 1950s.

We have a full compliment of Smokey Bears in our collection, from the first issue in the mid 1950s to some of the recent models. Doris could not resist the temptation to do a transplant operation on one of our earlier Smokeys and

A talking Smokey Bear poster.

able to respond to the human voice and mumble a like number of syllables to anyone speaking within his range. By repeating numbers, we managed to get our A.G. to count up to eight. Admittedly, you do have to speak rather rapidly when you want him to repeat in succession each number from one to eight, but it can be done. Since A.G.'s introduction several years ago, more advanced micro technology has allowed the introduction of talking teddies that do not just mumble, but actually repeat your words. When we packed our teddies to be photographed for this book, we discovered that A.G. would even talk back while packed in a big box, so we took the liberty of forewarning our photographer that if he heard some strange sounds coming from one of the boxes in his studio, not to be concerned because it was just A.G. trying to get his attention.

With the advances being made in computer technology and micro miniaturization, it is not too farfetched to believe that within the foreseeable future, someone will produce dolls and teddy bears that not only speak, but give plausable responses to questions given them. Think of how exciting it will be a hundred years from now to discover an "old" teddy with this capability and to learn first hand what kind of a life he and his owner lived! Then we may well say, "If only they would stop talking!"

put a voice box in him from a later model. We now have a one-of-a-kind Smokey Bear that responds to the pull of his string with appropriate sayings about preventing forest fires. We also have a rather unique talking poster that is simply a flat piece of cardboard with Smokey Bear's likeness on the face of it, with a voice box and cord attached to the back. It was commercially made that way and it says, "Talking Poster" on the face.

If you can allow a little latitude in your thinking, we can classify teddy bears with music boxes in them as "talking teddies." They are talking in a musical statement but they are certainly saying (or singing) something. On one of my business trips for a previous employer, I found myself in Dallas, Texas. I wanted to bring something home to Doris that was representative of this great state so I found a special teddy bear in the world-famous Neimann Marcus Department Store that was properly attired in a cowboy hat and bolo tie identified with the Neimann Marcus name. He was a musical teddy that played, "Deep In The Heart of Texas."

About five years ago a clever teddy bear producer marketed a talking teddy bear dressed in a business suit, shirt and tie, and called him the Executive Teddy Bear. He had a pull string and would offer such encouraging phrases as "You're a born Leader...Teddy Knows," and other words of encouragement to a harried executive. It was clever enough to capture a lot of free publicity on television, which must have done wonders for sales of the little guy. Two of them managed to find their way into our collection.

One of my all-time favorites is a teddy called, "A.G." This unique bear does not really say anything, except he is

15in (38cm) Texas teddy bear.

This talking teddy bear has several reassuring statements for the harried executive.

A.G. is a teddy that mumbles back everything you say to him.

Button in the Ear

A charming Steiff from the 1950s, 25in (64cm).

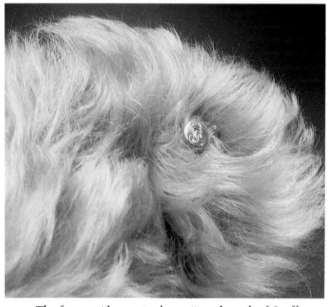

The famous "button-in-the-ear" trademark of Steiff.

What is the first thing a prospective buyer of an antique teddy bear looks for? A button in the ear, of course, a positive indication that the teddy is a Steiff, the famous German bear-making company whose antique teddies are setting world record prices both at auction and at private sales. Would it come as a surprise to you to discover that a small metal button in the ear of a teddy turns out to be of French origin? It did to us.

In 1985 we visited the popular Glendale Toy Show held in January every year. We were just starting our personal appearance tour in California and managed to find enough time to take in this respected show. It is the largest antique toy show beyond the St. Charles, Illinois, show we have ever attended and you can choose from a huge variety of toys and advertising antiques offered by dealers from all over the nation. Teddy bears are not neglected at this show and are offered in abundance. We even made a purchase from a dealer from Holland at this show.

It was at a California dealer's booth that we found a teddy with his button in the ear in place and we were informed by

Polar bear by Deans of England, 18in (46cm).

This polar bear carries his metal I.D. tag in his right foot. Ouch!

Button-in-ear of French bear carries initials "F.A.D.A.P." We are seeking more information on this company.

A rare French teddy bear, circa 1920s, 14in (36cm).

the dealer that it was a French teddy bear. Closer examination revealed the initials "F.A.D.A.P." It was an exciting find and there was no question that the teddy had found a new home. Since we were in California at the time, we were able to share our find with Paul and Rosemary Volpp. It turns out that the only other example by this French company that we have seen is in the Volpp collection. Their French bear has a cloth tag in addition to his button and it gives the origin as Divonne, France. We estimate the age of our French-button teddy as being from the 1920s.

Sometimes the button may not be as obvious, as was the case with a Chad Valley rabbit we sold to Rosemary Volpp a few years ago. She called excitedly a week or so later to ask us if we were aware that the bunny had a Chad Valley button imbedded deep inside his ear. I confessed that I had missed it, but she could feel free to send along an extra $50.00 if she wanted to.

Chad Valley used a printed tin button on some of their teddy bears as well, as is evidenced in a striking little mohair teddy bear we found in a charming little shop in the southern part of England. We discovered several old teddy bears in his shop, including a clown teddy with a Chad Valley printed button in his ear. By far the largest number of antique teddy bears do not come with any form of identification so it is always an added bonus to find one that has been marked in some way by the maker.

The button or tag may not always be located in the ear of the bear. We have a large polar bear that was made by the famous Deans Company of Great Britain. Our Dean's polar

bear has a metal button implanted in the bottom of his foot. We have seen another copy of this bear with a cloth tag carrying the company's name. I suspect that they may have identified them with both cloth tag and button. Or perhaps they ran out of cloth tags at one point and used buttons until a new supply could be obtained. Early bear makers were

A unique British teddy, circa 1930s, 12in (31cm).

A tin button identifies this teddy as made by Chad Valley.

frugal by necessity and I am convinced that a practice of substituting identification buttons or tags did indeed take place if it was necessary to keep production going.

Now that we are aware of other firms that identified their teddy bears with a button in the ear, we have to wonder when we receive a picture of a teddy bear with an accompanying letter that informs us that the bear in question has his button. Most of the time we can identify a Steiff from across the room because of the distinctive style, but no longer can we say that a button in the ear is positive proof it is made by Steiff.

There was certainly no question with a very large (25in [64cm]) Steiff that came through our door in the summer of 1988. This excellent specimen grew up with his original owner, Joseph Austin, of Fremont, Michigan. The teddy bear, along with a number of other Steiff animals, were purchased at the famous F.A.O. Schwarz toy store in New York City in the mid 1950s. Joseph's teddy now enjoys his residence in our front showcase, sharing the lower half with other large teddy bears.

Teddy, the Salesman

Once the teddy bear was established as a popular figure in our lives in the early 1900s, it did not take long for manufactureres to capitalize on this popularity by including a bear in their promotions. I spent a number of years in the field of advertising and can appreciate the power of tying in a product with a teddy bear. Doris and I keep our eyes out for these promotional teddies and usually add them to our collection. They are most often reasonably priced, requiring several labels of a given product along with a few dollars. They are also somewhat limited in production, more often than not offered for a specific time period. We limit our purchases to those promotional teddies that have the product name with the bear so that we will always know who promoted the teddy. We feel the value is lost if it is simply a mass produced teddy bear that is offered by a manufacturer of some product, with no identity on the bear itself.

A recent acquisition is the cute little blue teddy bear offered by the makers of Aunt Jemima frozen waffles. He is 14in (36cm) tall and comes dressed as a cook, presumably preparing waffles for breakfast. We checked the tag on ours and discovered it was produced for them by North American Bear Company. Anyone who collects their popular character bears will certainly want to add this little fellow to their collection. You will likely find them turning up at teddy bear shows.

Snuggles is a teddy bear that was produced as a result of an advertising campaign that made him a star. We have them in two sizes. Celestial Seasonings Tea makers have used a sleepy little bear on their colorful tin boxes for a number of years. We were most pleased when they offered the bear as a promotion a few years ago, and even more pleased when we received him and discovered it was a faithful likeness to the teddy on their tea tins.

One of the best made bears in our collection of advertising bears is one that was produced in Canada. It was a promotional piece that was obtainable by purchasing a cleaning product called Pine Sol. This big guy is a soft, cuddly bear. He, like most of the advertising bears, is not jointed. Because of the need to keep their costs to a minimum so that the buyer can obtain the teddy for a low price, most of the bears in this category are non jointed types made in acrylic materials.

Sugar Bear, the Post Cereal teddy, is made almost pancake style, cutting an outline top and bottom and sewing the two pieces together. This helps to keep costs down to a minimum so the premium can be marketed widely at an extremely low price. Panadol, a children's aspirin, has a cute little baby panda bear in a diaper. Since Doris has a fondness for pandas, it was a foregone conclusion that this little panda would join the collection.

Some of the promotional teddies come in appropriate outfits, such as the charming Del Monte Teddy that comes in

14in (36cm) premium teddy produced by the North American Bear Company for Aunt Jemima.

his bib overalls with Del Monte printed on them or the cute little Fiddle Faddle Teddy, who wears overalls and carries a cloth fiddle. The product is a coated caramel corn and with my sweet tooth, it was no problem coming up with the required box labels.

Other advertising teddy bears that deserve mentioning are the vast array of bears that appear every Christmas season, where you can buy the bear for a low price if you purchase so many dollars worth of gift merchandise from the department store carrying the promotion. The first time it was offered, it created record sales for the chain stores that came up with the concept. Because it was so successful, the following year it had many other stores participating and each year it has grown, although it may have reached saturation this past year because many of the stores had teddies left after Christmas.

Because the teddy bear has magic appeal to children and adults, he will continue to be used as an important promotional tool to sell a vast array of merchandise the world over.

Clever television commercials created a demand for Snuggles, made in several sizes.

Excellent quality teddy made for Pine Sol in Canada.

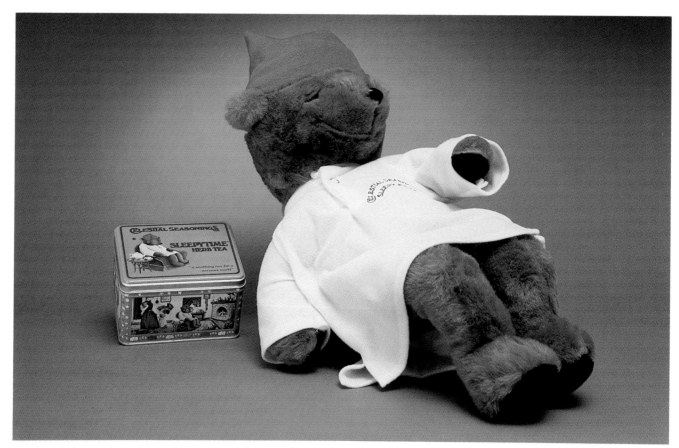

Celestial Seasonings Tea Company had a teddy produced in the likeness of the bear on their clever packages.

Non-jointed teddy made for Post Cereal, 15in (38cm).

This Panadol Panda wears a diaper, 10in (25cm).

Brawny Bear wears his Del Monte big overalls, 9in (23cm).

Fiddle Faddle Bear is ready for a hoedown. He comes complete with a stuffed fiddle.

Send in the Clowns

A delightful tiny clown, 3½in (9cm), by Artist Dickie Harrison.

On my list of "to do's" some day is to become a clown. I could have been persuaded at one time in my life to enroll in the famous clown college, followed by a stint with Barnum and Bailey's Circus. Unfortunately, a wife and family, a real college and a career got in the way. The smell of the grease-paint and the roar of the crowd is still there in my mind. Maybe that is why I am a pushover for a clown teddy bear.

Clowns and teddy bears seem to be a natural combination. Children (and big kids like me) adore them both so why not combine them into one great package? Many of the leading teddy bear manufacturers have done just that through the years. Donna Harrison and Dottie Ayers have managed to find two old clowns for our collection over the past few years. One is a marvelous 13in (33cm) German teddy clown with an orange and pink mohair body and a white felt clown hat. They brought it back to us from one of their European buying trips. Donna also discovered a pink and blue antique teddy clown during one of the bus trips into Pennsylvania antique country that have become a follow-up to the Baltimore teddy bear convention and show each fall. Doris and I were on the same bus but when it stops at one of the big outdoor markets and 50 teddy bear collectors pour out of the bus, scattering in all directions, it is almost impossible to be the first at every table. The 1930s teddy clown had just a small worn spot in front, so Doris managed to find an appropriate lace decoration to cover his bad spot and add to his clown decor.

One of the greatest clown teddy finds we have is a 1913 original Steiff Bar Dolly. Actually, his body is original, but the head is by Carrousel by Michaud. We found the red mohair body at an outdoor antique market and since it was only $10.00, we decided to gamble that some day we might find his red mohair head. We were surprised to discover him on a series of post cards showing early Steiff teddy bears, and even more surprised to learn that his head was white mohair

with an orange ruff around his neck. We could not wait to make him a new head of white mohair and produce a orange yarn ruff. We know he is pleased because teddy bears like to "get a-head!"

We do a teddy bear making seminar in Chesaning, Michigan, twice a year. It is attended by 100 enthusiastic bear makers and everyone leaves with a completed teddy bear. A few years ago the project was a clown teddy with a maroon and green body and a gold acrylic head. It was fun going around at the end of the day and seeing a hundred different teddies, all made with the same pattern, but finished by a hundred different bear makers.

We have a small 6½in (17cm) teddy that Doris made for me as a gift way back when and we found a neat little knitted clown outfit that fits him perfectly. Our smallest clown, however, was handcrafted by Dickie Harrison, one of the most talented and delightful miniaturists in the country. This little black and white clown bear is a mere 3½in (9cm) tall. We have well over a dozen of Dickie's fascinating little teddy bears and we cannot seem to get enough of them.

Clown teddy bears are great fun to display because you can have them performing in a three-ring circus, pouring into or out of a roadster or coming along in parade formation. Some of our clowns were designed to be clowns by the maker and some are teddy bears that were just ordinary teddies that were transformed by an imaginative costume. Regardless of their origin, they can add a large dose of cheer to an otherwise ordinary collection.

A 1930s clown teddy found in Germany, 13in (33cm).

The body of this clown bear is made half in white mohair and half in gold mohair. Lace decorations added to cover worn spot. 16in (41cm).

A 1915 Steiff clown with restored head. Identified on post card back as Bar Dolly. 17in (43cm).

Original Bar Dolly with current Steiff reproduction.

13in (33cm) clown made by participants in semi annual Carrousel bear making seminar.

This tiny teddy 6½in (16cm) was transformed into a clown by a well-knitted suit. Bear by Doris Michaud. The suit was a gift from Jane Servinski.

Send in the clowns.

Section II

Following the introduction of our first book, *Bears Repeating, Stories Old Teddy Bears Tell*, a few years ago, we received so many encouraging letters about the stories of teddy bears and their original owners that we instituted a regular column in *Teddy Bear and friends*® magazine titled "Bears Repeating." In addition to sharing stories of some of the unique teddy bears in our Carrousel Museum Collection, we strive to share stories of special teddies in collections of arctophiles the world over. We are always looking for humorous or touching stories about teddy bears and we would love to hear from you, our readers.

We are pleased to include a reprint of our columns in this section.

The Royal Birthmark

We would be hard-pressed to choose our favorite teddy bear show or convention because each has its own distinctive appeal. Linda and Wally Mullins' January show in San Diego is high on our list, not only because of the exceptional weather (Michigan has a tendency to be rather "white" in January), but also because of its sheer size and offerings, and primarily because it gives us a chance to renew our friendship with the Mullins, two of the most sharing people it has been our pleasure to meet.

Rated in the top show conventions in the country is the great magic of Teddy Bears Convention in Baltimore, Maryland. The show (and subsequent convention) is guided by the capable hands of Donna Harrison.

We are always excited about the opening date of the Baltimore show because we can count on finding one or more treasures there; this past September show was no exception. Well-known doll and teddy bear dealer Richard Wright had just completed setting up his booth when we arrived on the scene. We left with several additions to our Museum Collection including one very special teddy. After our return to home base where we had time for closer inspection during the course of cleaning and some minor repairs, we discovered that one of our purchases was kin to the Duke of Portobello (see our first book, *Bears Repeating, Stories Old Teddy Bears Tell*, page 58).

What first appeared to be a repair on the side of the head turned out to be part of the original pattern. It is a seam in the mohair running from a point near the "Adam's apple" back toward the ear. It became obvious it was not a repair when the same seam was discovered on the opposite side of the head.

We were suspicious of a relationship to the Duke of

Illustration 1. 28in (71cm) Duke of Portobello and his long-lost 24in (61cm) sister.

Portobello not only because of style similarities, but because of the cardboard sole inserts in the feet on both bears. Proof of the relationship was confirmed when the same seemingly out-of-place seam was found on the Duke of Portobello! Why the extra seam in the design? We can only speculate that perhaps it allowed the maker to create a different shape of the head.

Comparing the Duke and the second bear to other British bears in our collection by known makers, we have ruled out Merrythought, Deans and Chad Valley. Some indications point to Alpha Farnell. Due to the unusual seams on both sides of the head, we are certain that someone will have a similar bear in their collection and know the origin. Meanwhile, we need to bestow a title on the Duke of Portobello's long-lost sister. Perhaps some time spent at the library researching English nobility might prove fruitful.

A "Genuine" Friend

Illustration 1. Angela Grosse Hetzel at age four in 1907 with Genuine. Photograph courtesy of Mary Doudna.

Illustration 2. Mary Doudna and Genuine. Mary is Mrs. Hetzel's daughter. Hobby House Press, Inc. photograph.

Our personal appearance tours bring us in touch with many warm and sharing teddy bear collectors from coast to coast. When we are doing an appearance in a shop, it is not always easy to determine who the employees are and who the customers are because teddy bear people are often so quick to lend a helping hand. Mary Doudna and her husband, Lon, make their home in Stevens Point, Wisconsin. Mary is one of those friendly and outgoing people who does not wait to be asked to lend a helping hand; she usually recognizes the need, then offers to do it. At a teddy bear show in Toledo, for example, Mary volunteered to watch our booth while we were doing a bear-making seminar. Later the same day I spotted her helping out in another booth.

Mary's bear collection, which numbers in the 500 range, is as wide and varied as Mary's interests. Her collection even extends beyond bears to rabbits. Mary says that rabbits are her first love and when you meet Holly, her pet Holland lop-eared rabbit who has the run of the house, you will be convinced the statement is in fact true.

It is always hard to choose a favorite teddy in a collection but that task would be relatively easy for Mary. The honor would most likely go to Genuine, a charming 12in (30cm) Steiff teddy from 1907. This bear belonged to Mary's mother, Angela Grosse Hetzel, who was born in 1903. As a child, Mary remembers the bear being kept in an oak bookcase with sliding doors. She had little or no interest in it at the time as she had her own stuffed animals.

In 1969 her mother decided it was time someone got some use out of the bear so she tearfully presented it to Mary's daughter, Kelly, during a summer visit to Doudna's home in Ohio — their residence at the time. Kelly lugged the bear around for about six years; then it was relegated to a shelf as Kelly's interests changed. It was Kelly who came up with the name "Genuine" for this family treasure. She felt it looked like the original Pooh drawings so she called it Genuine Pooh. The name later was shortened to Genuine.

Since Mary's interest in teddy bears has remained strong, she is temporary guardian; however, Kelly is quick to point out to anyone who shows an interest that Genuine belongs to her!

Mary's mother is still living and asks about the bear frequently. She is thrilled that her valuable childhood treasure is so cherished. Genuine was pictured in Peter Bull's last book, *Hug of Bears*. He is shown on page six, but is incorrectly listed as belonging to Hazel Pollock.

It is poetic justice that a well-loved teddy bear named Geuine resides with Mary Doudna — a genuine friend and fellow collector.

Teddy Bear Bread
The Mystery is Solved

One of the true joys of writing are the follow-up letters received from teddy bear collectors and makers from around the world. It is particularly gratifying to receive information that sheds light on a previous mystery. Such is the case with a letter received regarding our article, "Teddy Bear Bread Bear." (See *Teddy Bear and friends*® magazine, January/February 1986, page 73.)

You may recall the story about the giant 40in (101cm) teddy bear that was believed to have come from the Teddy Bear Bread Company of Detroit, Michigan, in the early 1900s. It is owned by two delightful sisters in Saginaw, Michigan, and has been in their family since that time. Shortly after the article was published, we received a charming letter from Dr. Phyllis Gore of Wisenheimer, North

Wash Day In Teddy Bear Land

Wagner's
Teddy Bear Bread
Every Bite a Delight

1913	**FEBRUARY**					1913
SUN	MON	TUE	WED	THU	FRI	SAT
6TH NEW M.	14TH FIRST Q.	20TH FULL M.	27TH LAST			1
2	3	4	5	6	7	8
9	10	11	12	13	14	15
16	17	18	19	20	21	22
23	24	25	26	27	28	

FEBRUARY — SECOND MONTH

Illustration 1. The girl in this Teddy Bear Bread calendar from 1913 is the sister of Dr. Phyllis Gore, Virginia Wagner Schindler. Photograph courtesy of Dr. Phyllis Gore.

product called "Teddy Bear Bread." Dr. Gore recalled her dad often telling her about the Teddy Bear Bread campaign and how successful it was. Other promotions were tried over the years, including one for Bluebird Bread, but none matched the success of Teddy Bear Bread. Some of Dr. Gore's happiest moments were the trips to the bakery, sitting on the bar stools connected to a long counter area, enjoying a glass of milk with the special baked goods of the day. She recalls a huge teddy bear resting amidst the mugs in the mirrored background. Between his legs sat a loaf of Teddy Bear Bread!

Dr. Gore recalls that her grandfather, a frugal man, had only five of the large bears to use in various display areas. She speculates that they may have been given to friends or customers, and laments that fact that she was not able to acquire one. About a dozen of the horse-drawn Teddy Bear Bread Wagon toys (see the cover, January/February 1986 *Teddy Bear and friends*) were given by the Wagner Baking Company as part of the promotion to the stores that were old standby customers.

One treasured keepsake from the bakery Dr. Gore was able to acquire is a 1913 calendar. The child in the picture washing her teddy bears is Dr. Gore's late sister, Virginia Wagner Schindler. Note the slogan "Every bite a delight" on the calendar, which matches the Teddy Bear Bread pin in the Carrousel Museum Collection.

Dr. Gore's letter concludes with the following nostalgia. "While visiting Detroit in October, I [was able to] take a picture of the Wagner Baking Company on Woodward Avenue. The company name is etched in stone at the top of the building. The place is empty now, but the memories were rekindled momentarily, and I honestly believe I still could smell Dad's hot cinnamon buns — a nostalgic fragrance of my past. Perhaps it is a good thing I could not get in the building. Maybe I would have envisioned Teddy Bears and Bluebirds!"

Dr. Gore and her cousin, Mae Spitzer, were subsequently able to visit our shop and museum and meet with the Teddy Bear Bread Bear and its current owner. We are most grateful to Dr. Gore for sending the photograph of the calendar and for her initial response to the article. We are also grateful her son, David, is a bear collector, for it was this connection that prompted Dr. Gore to pick up the magazine and discover the article about the Teddy Bear Bread Bear.

Illustration 2. Alice Fallahay Pedlow, at age ten, with the Teddy Bear Bread Bear. Photograph courtesy of the Pedlow family.

Carolina. She had picked up a copy of the magazine at a doll boutique and when she read the story, she was able to solve the mystery of the Teddy Bear Bread Company.

Dr. Gore's grandfather, Edward Wagner, came from Bitt Burg, Germany, with his brothers and founded the Wagner Baking Company in Detroit in 1868. Her father, George John Wagner, became involved with the bakery at an early age. One of the sales promotions of the early 1900s was a

Love — Pass It On

This is a love story involving three people with a shared love of teddy bears. The central character is a white 13in (33cm) Steiff teddy with a blank button. The first person whose life he touched was a charming lady named Mary Bliss who received the bear as a Christmas gift at age four. The year was 1905 and the place was Burlington, Vermont. Mary had a number of dolls as a child, but teddy was always her security blanket and companion. Her mother stored the bear in a trunk when Mary grew beyond childhood and there he remained for over 70 years, discovered only a few years ago. Last year Mary had two needs to address. One was a financial one and the other was a desire to find a loving home for her childhood treasure. She knew that fine old teddy bears were commanding respectable prices so she opted to sell him through Christie's Auction in New York in 1987.

Teddy was about to touch the life of a second person. It would have been difficult not to take notice of teddy because in addition to being a blank button Steiff in mint condition, he also shared the cover of the auction book with a fine quality doll featured in the sale. Anxiously awaiting the sale and the assortment of teddy bears being offered was Donna Harrison.

Our prized teddy was destined to join Donna's stock of quality bruins. To make it an even more exciting purchase, who should approach Donna after the sale but Mary Bliss! It seems she was concerned about the final destination of her lifetime companion. Donna promised to find a good home and loving guardian for this teddy and acquired the former owner's name and address for future reference.

Donna could have chosen a proper collector from perhaps hundreds of people on her list but fate has a way of bringing just the right person together with just the right teddy. Enter our third person whose life was to be touched by teddy. Karen Silverstein is an attorney from Ithaca, New York. She has been collecting stuffed animals for most of her life and credits her grandmother for instilling a love of collecting in her. She fondly recalls frequent trips to F.A.O. Schwarz, the famous toy store in New York City, where her grandmother would buy her a Steiff animal.

After Karen completed law school, she discovered (or perhaps rediscovered) teddy bears and started a collection of handmade teddies. Antique teddy bears entered her life when she attended an auction of old bears and made her first purchase of a previously loved teddy, a charming early American bear. Since that day, she has focused on antique teddy bears. Karen has added another dimension to her love of teddy bears by sharing them with the very people whose lives they were meant to touch — children. Mary supplies teddies to a local family court judge who not only uses them to soothe children with whom she works, but frequently

Illustration 1. Jeffrey, a 13in (33cm) Steiff with a blank button. Photograph courtesy of Karen Silverstein.

Illustration 2. Jeffrey and his original owner, Mary Bliss. Photograph courtesy of Karen Silverstein.

Illustration 3. Jeffrey sharing the front cover of the Christie's auction catalog. Photograph courtesy of Christie's.

gives them to children who do not have toys. One of Karen's greatest joys is to drive down the street and see a child with one of her teddy bears being dragged lovingly along.

Destiny, or some force beyond our recognition, brought Karen and Donna together and "Jeffrey" (Karen's name for the Steiff teddy) has taken up residence in Karen's collection since that day. She has subsequently corresponded with Mary Bliss on several occasions and will undoubtedly continue to write her on occasion to reassure her that teddy continues to share his love.

Tracking Teddy Bears in Britain

A casual remark by a friend started us making plans for a trip that took us to Great Britain in search of teddy bears. Our good friends and business associates, Bill and Rosemary Hayes, were debating what they should do to celebrate their 25th anniversary and they asked what we did for ours. "That's simple," I replied. "We made a trip to England and you should do the same. In fact, you should take us along as guides since we have been there four times.

That comment was early in the year and on August 9th the four of us left Detroit bound for a two-week sojourn through England. The trip was of necessity a business trip but fortunately, our business is strongly oriented around teddy bears so we can combine business with pleasure. We knew we had chosen the right airline when the captain announced, as we approached London, that he was being ably assisted by his teddy bear, Gary Gatwick! He invited one and all to tour the cockpit after landing and he would introduce us. Unfortunately, too many people took him up on the offer so we opted to get on with our tour instead.

Our first five days were spent in London tracking down teddy bears at the famous street markets (Portobello Road, Camden Passage, Bermundsey) and through a host of daily antique markets. We did manage to take in some of the more interesting tourist sights (Tower of London, Westminster Abbey and other places), but always checking first to see if there was a teddy bear shop or an antique market in the vicinity. We were modestly successful in acquiring a few teddies at Portobello Road and Bermundsey markets, but the bears we purchased were neither rare nor inexpensive. We can safely say that the interest in antique teddies is nearly as strong in Great Britain as it is here.

We picked up a rental car at Heathrow Airport and headed north. Driving on the left side is a great thrill that everyone should experience. A small sign placed on the dashboard saying "Think Left" is a helpful reminder. Bill and I took turns at the wheel and we really only got in trouble once, when another American tourist was coming at us on the wrong side!

Two days spent in Edinburgh, Scotland, did not produce any antique teddy bears; however, it did give us the opportunity to attend their famous Military Tattoo at Edinburgh Castle. It runs nightly for about three weeks in August and features drum and pipe bands from all over the world. If you love bagpipe music, you will be delighted with the Tattoo.

Our lodging consisted primarily of England's famous bed and breakfast establishments where you are literally renting a room in a private home. It is more economical than hotels and it gives you a chance to learn more about a given area from a resident. We spent several days in the popular Lake District in the northwest part of England. We were forewarned that it rained there most of the time and it did, indeed, but generally it was a light shower for half an hour

Illustration 1. An English miss clutching her handmade teddy and enjoying a sweet. Is that Doris attempting to snatch it away? Terry Michaud photograph.

Illustration 2. The Professor welcomes Me Too, a 12in (30cm) Alpha Farnell Teddy, circa 1930s. Terry Michaud photograph.

Illustration 3. Hello, Hello! Is there anybody there? It took all three of us to carry Doris away! Terry Michaud photograph.

followed by periods of sun. The small villages have a number of antique shops but again, the selection of teddy bears was limited.

Our first break in locating teddies came in a small town called Witney, just west of Oxford. We had been told of a teddy bear shop there that had antique teddies as well as contemporary bears. The name of the shop is Teddy Bears and, although half of the shop is devoted to miscellaneous antiques and collectibles, the other half offers a selection of artist and manufactured teddy bears. I found a charming lead figure of a teddy made in France. After brief introductions, we were escorted to the teddy room upstairs and we found a variety of antique teddies to choose from. The selection was unfortunately somewhat limited because the charming couple that operate the shop had just returned from a show where a good portion of their antique teddy bears went to other homes.

We selected half a dozen that needed further consideration. One small bear caught Doris' eye and she set him back on the shelf, only to retrieve him several times. She said later the bear kept saying, "Me too, me too" and so "Me Too" came home to join the Carrousel collection. Doris had experienced some apprehension about riding in a car being driven on the wrong side so she decided to keep her mind occupied by knitting a mohair sweater for Me Too. His "worry" sweater turned out great and was a big help in limiting her back-seat driving.

The latter portion of our Brisith tour was spent in the southern part of the country, in and around the beautiful seaside town of Brighton. There you will find a section called the Lanes, where blocks of fascinating shops are located in a maze of narrow corridors. We did locate a marvelous shop that specializes in dolls and teddy bears; unfortunately it was closed. The sign indicated that she sold to the Trade and to serious collectors so I presume an appointment would be required.

It took a good deal of work and driving over 1400 miles, but we did manage to come back with an even dozen antique teddy bears. We also came back with fond memories of the beautiful gardens homeowners keep and the delightful sweets they make.

I think we will have to make another trip sometime just to see what was inside that shop that was closed.

The Blitz

Illustration 1. Eleanor Lorentz (standing) holding Cecily's teddy bear while her sister, Jeanne Fontaine, looks on. Terry Michaud photograph.

Toledo, Ohio, and London, England, are thousands of miles from each other. Yet they were drawn together in a number of ways when we participated in the famous Hobby Center Toys annual Doll and Teddy Bear Show. It is undoubtedly the biggest show of its kind in the world. The Savino family celebrated its tenth show in the fall of 1988 and there were artists, designers and producers representing most of the major companies in the doll and teddy bear world. With these two hobbies right at the top in popularity with collectors, you can imagine the thousands of eager teddy bear and doll enthusiasts who come from all over the United States to attend this show.

England was well represented, with officials from Merrythought, House of Nisbet and Canterbury Bears attending and showing their newest creations. We always thoroughly enjoy the opportunity of spending some time with our British friends, whether it be at this marvelous show or on their own turf in England. Perhaps one of the reasons we

hold our British friends in such high esteem is due to the recognition of the determination and courage they displayed during World War II. We can only imagine the horror of the daily bombings that took place there, and how terrifying it must have been for young and old alike. Which brings us to our story.

This is the story of a little British girl named Cecily. More to the point, it is the story of Cecily's teddy bear. We learned of this poignant story from Eleanor Lorentz from Adrian, Michigan, and her sister, Jeanne Fontaine, of Galesburg, Michigan. Both sisters were visiting the Toledo show and brought along a charming but well-worn Merrythought teddy bear. It was easily identified by his original Merrythought button in his ear. The sisters had shown it to Oliver Holmes at the Merrythought booth and learned that this particular bear was produced from 1933 until World War II began.

The teddy bear was identified in another very special

Illustration 2. Cecily's teddy bear in a recently acquired antique doctor's satchel. Terry Michaud photograph.

RIGHT: Illustration 3. Cecily Craddock's teddy bear with the name written on the chest. Terry Michaud photograph.

way, for written on a ribbon sewn to his chest was the name "Cecily Craddock." Jeanne discovered the teddy in Grant's Antique Mall in Galesburg in mid August. Her parents, Zell and Hallie Scamehorn, of Richmond, Michigan, were told about the bear, and a decision was made to buy the bear and give it to Jeanne as an early Christmas present. It was a special gift, indeed, because the Scamehorns also collect teddy bears!

Eleanor's contribution was a story she composed to go with the teddy bear and it tells the story of Cecily and her bear much better than we could hope to. She composed the story with the facts at hand and her love of teddy bears. Her story follows verbatim.

"August 25, 1988. Cecily Craddock was a little girl in London during World War II and I was her bear. A war is a terrible thing, and its icy fingers reach out and leave a mark on every family. History tells us London was bombed 104 straight nights.

"At the sound of the siren, Cecily grabbed me up, and off we went to the air raid shelter, feeling secure in each other's arms.

"I carried her name right on my foot, but we got separated anyway, and I was left alone in the bomb shelter with lots of time to wonder about Cecily.

"Then one day in 1942 a lady found me still waiting in the shelter. (Bears are like that — patient and faithful.) She gave me a hug like Cecily used to. I lived with her until 1988 when she, too went away, and there was an estate sale.

"A dealer found something appealing about my threadbare condition, and she placed me in a big store window, in a wagon, right up close where I could watch for a friendly face, and that's how I came to be an early Christmas gift.

"Cecily would have wanted it that way."

Roy and Shirley

Illustration 1. Grandpa's Baby, a fully-jointed acrylic teddy bear that stands at 11in (28cm). Terry Michaud photograph.

Roy and Shirley Howey of Phoenix, Arizona, are two extraordinary teddy bear artists we met several years ago. They are active members of the Phoenix Teddy Bear Club that sponsors a delightful teddy bear show every January and one that we include on our winter tour.

Both Roy and Shirley collect teddy bears (with some 500 plus bears in their collection) and they have five children and 14 grandchildren to keep them occupied during their spare time. Quite often, the bear maker wife teaches her husband the art, but in this case it was Roy who taught Shirley how to make bears. Both Roy and Shirley have their own individual style. Roy makes jointed acrylic teddies from 11in (28cm) up to 25in (64cm) and Shirley concentrates on miniatures. She works almost exclusively in mohair and her largest teddy is 6in (15cm) tall. They sell their teddies by mail order and at a limited number of shows. Shirley supplies some shops as well.

Shirley's bear making career began in 1986, but Roy started on teddy bears in 1984 as therapy. Roy took medical retirement from his engineering job with Mobil Oil Corporation in 1972 and underwent open heart surgery in 1974. As a form of therapy, he began making quilts and then got started producing teddy bears. In 1985 they discovered Roy had multiple myeloma but fortunately, his cancer is in remission today. Roy's health problems were not over yet because in 1986 his kidneys failed; today he must go to the hospital three days a week for dialysis. He is on oxygen about 60% of the time. It is an absolute miracle he is able to make bears at all, but Roy says he sews because it takes his mind off his health problems. The more he hurts, the more he sews.

Up until this year, Roy made teddies selling in the $40.00 to $100.00 price range. The nurses at the hospital where Roy spends so much of his time are very familiar with "Grandpa's Teddy Bears," as he calls them, but Roy knew that many of the nurses were single parents trying to make ends meet and he decided they should have one of his bears for their children to enjoy. Therefore, he introduced Grandpa's Babies. These are fully-jointed 11in (28cm) teddies with safety eyes and plastic noses. He sells them for $20.00. Needless to say, they have made a big hit not only with the nurses, but many arctophiles as well. They were a complete sellout at the Phoenix show in January 1989.

Roy has some very definite thoughts about teddy bears. He states emphatically that blue-eyed bears are girls, while brown-eyed bears can be either boys or girls. Roy is also quick to demonstrate his proper method for hugging a bear. Roy makes a charming rabbit he calls "Funny Bunny," and sheep are made as well. Shirley has called on her quilt-making abilities and now produces adorable miniature quilts.

We look forward each year to seeing Roy and Shirley at the Phoenix show and to adding one or two new Grandpa's Bears to our collection. Every time I see his teddy or his Funny Bunny, it reminds me of what an important role attitude plays in our lives.

Illustration 2. Roy and Shirley Howey. Shirley is holding one of her miniature quilts and Roy is holding a Grandpa's Baby.'' Terry Michaud photograph.

Illustration 3. The Grandpa's Baby that joined our collection appropriately photographed with a symbol of Arizona. Terry Michaud photograph.

A Bear from Budapest

Illustration 1. A 19½in (47cm) Steiff teddy bear discovered in an antique shop in Budapest, Hungary. Terry Michaud photograph.

This is a story of a magnificent early Steiff teddy bear named Lyda Rose who spent much of her lifetime in Budapest, Hungary. Her story really starts in Madison, Wisconsin, where her owner, Karen Schwarz, lives with her husband, Dan. Karen is an administrator for a large cancer research center at the University of Wisconsin. Needless to say, she is also a devoted arctophile.

Karen began collecting teddy bears in 1980. It started out innocently enough, with the purchase of a small basic brown bear she saw in the window of a shop. The collection grew slowly, until Karen found herself employed part time at a teddy bear shop that opened near her home. The shop owner, Gene Allen, became a good friend and together, they started a Teddy Bear Collectors' Club in Madison. The club became affiliated with Good Bears of the World, the organization that places teddies in hospitals and other places needing them.

In late June of 1988, Karen joined an enthusiastic group of doll and teddy bear collectors on a European tour. This is an annual tour that is conducted by Peter Kalinke, the U.S. representative of the Gebrüder Hermann company, one of the leading producers of fine bears and other plush animals from Germany. Peter has been a good friend of ours for a number of years, and I know of no one who is more knowledgeable about the German doll and teddy bear cottage

industry than he is. It is one of the reasons Peter is in demand as a speaker at teddy bear conventions all over the country. Peter's tours are always a sellout, due not only to his great knowledge, but also because he has such a warm, open personality and people welcome the opportunity to be in his company.

Peter's many contacts allowed those on the trip a unique view into the cottage industries of Europe. The 1988 group was made up of 43 people of varied backgrounds, including shop owners, teddy bear lovers, doll enthusiasts and other collectors. Peter's lovely wife, Ana, and his daughter, Maria, also joined the tour. The tour started in Frankfurt, West Germany, and included visits to a number of doll factories and teddy bear producers as well as a host of flea markets where some hidden treasures were found. You did not have to be a doll and bear collector to enjoy this tour because there were ample opportunities for shopping in delightful villages as well as visits to many historical castles and the opportunity to see glassblowers and other artisans at work.

The tour passed through upper Bavaria and into Austria. Karen found Vienna unbelievable and decided that three months in Vienna would not be enough, let alone three days. The group left Vienna and followed the Danube into Hungary and on to Budapest.

Even though the country is under Communist control,

Illustration 2. Lyda Rose speaks fluent Hungarian, a bit of German, and is now enrolled in an English course at the University of Wisconsin. Terry Michaud photograph.

the group found Budapest an extremely charming city with beautiful bridges, parks, cathedrals and, of course, shopping. Karen and two other members of the group decided to do some shopping in the wonderful antique shops in the area. They entered one shop that offered a large selection of exquisite old Hungarian embroidery. The shopkeeper spoke Hungarian and the members of the tour spoke English so communication became a problem. Karen spoke limited German and the shop owner was able to converse some in German as well. An inquiry was made about teddy bears and the proprietor went into the back room and returned with Lyda Rose, a 19½in (47cm) early Steiff teddy. It was handed to one member of the tour who turned to Karen and said, "I'm not really a bear person. Are you interested?" Karen was more than interested, but a second problem arose. The matter of enough Hungarian currency stood in the way and the banks were already closed for the day. Karen did her best to let the owner know that she wold be back the next day for the teddy, then spent a restless night hoping that her limited German was clearly understood.

The next morning Karen arose early and hurried to the bank nearest the shop. When the shop opened, Karen was there, Hungarian forints in hand, ready to claim her treasure. Lyda Rose came out of the back room and was placed in a bag with her head out so she could see a bit of Budapest before leaving the country.

The border crossing posed a potential problem as Lyda Rose did not have a passport. An American teddy named A.G. was placed on top of the bag that Lyda Rose was in and she made it across the border without a problem.

Illustration 3. Lyda Rose in a christening gown from 1880. Terry Michaud photograph.

Lyda Rose has a place of honor in the Schwarz living room, wearing a dress and pinafore from 1880 that belonged to Karen's grandmother and was found in a trunk. It is a beautiful old lace christening gown and perfectly suits this wonderful teddy bear from Budapest.

Section III

In this section we have selected our three favorite stories from our first book, *Bears Repeating, Stories Old Teddy Bears Tell*, and we herewith retell them, offering details and background going back before the information previously presented. Names and places have been altered to protect the families involved. These accounts go back to retell the story....as it might have been.

In Memory of Tommy

Tommy's bear, 18in (46cm).

The dream of a lifetime came true for Thomas and Marian Stevens when their son, Tommy, was born in December of 1924. The Stevens had been married for nearly ten years and their desire to have a family led them through an endless parade of doctors. They even considered adoption but since they were poor, hard working farmers, they simply could not afford the legal help needed to proceed with an adoption. Marian and her husband, Tom, never gave up their

Tommy's bear and his collie dog pass the hours sitting in the sun, waiting for their master.

faith and they were blessed with a son when they least expected it. He was named Thomas Michael Junior and became known to all as Tommy.

Tommy was a frail little boy in his first few years but with the love his parents showered on him and the good, wholesome food typical of most farm homes, he soon grew into a healthy, active youngster. Tommy had two very close friends as companions. He had a collie dog named Lad and they were inseparable. It would be hard to say who had the strongest admiration for the other but the dog followed Tommy's every step as he did his daily chores before heading off to school. Lad waited patiently at the end of the road every afternoon until Tommy came into sight; then he made a bee line for his friend.

Tommy's second companion was a teddy bear given to him his first Christmas by his Uncle Ben, who worked in a large department store in Grand Rapids, Michigan. It was a struggle for Tommy's parents to make ends meet on their small farm land and they were only able to raise enough crops to feed themselves and a little extra for other necessities. Since there were precious few toys, Tommy loved his teddy bear even more. Lad was never jealous that he had to share Tommy's affections with a teddy bear. In fact, the dog seemed to enjoy the companionship of Tommy's bear as much as his master did.

As Tommy advanced in school, he no longer spent all his spare time with his dog and teddy because he was becoming too old for such things. The teddy bear took up residence on a chair in the corner of Tommy's bedroom and if Tommy was too busy with his chores or with a part time job he had at the local hardware store, Lad seemed to take on the responsibility of looking after teddy's welfare; he could often be found curled up on the rag rug in front of the chair in the bedroom.

Tommy was determined to maintain good grades in school because he dreamed of becoming a lawyer. He had an uncle on his mother's side that was an attorney in Chicago and he wanted to follow in his footsteps. He certainly did not want to take over the farm because he had seen his parents work long, hard hours with little reward.

Graduation was coming up fast and Tommy was busy trying to select a college. He would have to work part time to get through but with some help from his parents and from his uncle, it looked like his dream could become a reality. One thing stood between Tommy and his dream. It was World War II. Pearl Harbor had been struck the previous year and Tommy knew all along that his college would just have to wait. Several of his school buddies were planning to join the service and it seemed like the right thing for Tommy to do as well.

It was an emotional day that June when Tommy's dad drove him to the bus station. Lad and Tommy's teddy got to ride along but it was just too much for Tommy's mom to handle, so she stayed back at the farm. A brief reunion took place right after boot camp but it was all too short. Tommy spent the few days he had right at the farm, enjoying the company of his folks, his dog and his teddy.

Regular letters came to the farm from Tommy, always positive and always cheerful. Then the letters stopped and before Tommy's folks could enlist the aid of the Red Cross to check on his whereabouts, the telegram came. Tommy had been killed on the beaches at Normandy.

It was many months before Tommy's mother could bring herself to clean out his room. His teddy bear went into a trunk in the attic and it remained there until 1978, when a move from the farm to the city prompted Tommy's dad to take the bear to a friend in town who had an antique shop. We were in the right place at the right time, driving through the little farming community in Southwestern Michigan and stopping to check out yet another antique store. Tommy's bear has a very special place in our collection.

Me and My Shadow

Knitted bear and well-loved teddy found inside!

Maude and Edward Winston lived in the English village of Bodiam, just south of London. In 1924, their first child, Margaret was born. One of the gifts that arrived to celebrate her birth was a beautiful mohair jointed teddy bear. No one in the family remembers just who the gift was from, perhaps one of Maude's sisters who lived in London. At any rate, it was well loved right from the beginning and could often be found clutched in Baby Margaret's arms in her pram. Mr. Winston recalls that his little girl was fond of rubbing the teddy's mohair against her cheek and a small bald spot soon developed on teddy's head.

As a three year old, Margaret enjoyed the full attention of her loving parents, until her brother, Christopher, was born in 1927. Now she not only had to share the love of her parents, but her teddy bear was passed on to Christopher. Teddy got just as much attention with his new master but at times, it was a bit rough on him, as Christopher enjoyed throwing him around and when he got old enough to walk, the bear could often be seen dragged along behind him.

The only thing that saved poor teddy from the rough and tumble life he lived at the hands of Christopher was the birth of a third child in 1931. It was a baby girl named Alison and when she was old enough to play, teddy was reluctantly handed over to her by her brother.

Alison loved to dress her teddy and it did help to hide some of the bare patches that seemed to appear during Teddy's tenure with Christopher. In fact, Mrs. Winston remembers having to sew a patch or two on teddy where he was losing a little of his straw stuffing.

Mr. Winston worked for Brit Rail and his family got to travel a great deal. Frequent trips were made to London and during the short train ride, teddy was the center of sibling rivalry and ended up the unwilling participant in a three way tug-of-war. More patches were added, either sewn or glued in place to a body that was now almost completely devoid of original mohair. Mother Winston, no longer able to patch poor teddy, managed to persuade Alison to put him away. It took a special trade for a Golliwog to convince Alison to give her friend up but Mrs. Winston assured her daughter that teddy would be put away for safe keeping, and maybe some day he could be restored to health.

The years went by and the Winston children grew into young adulthood. Margaret married right after World War II and in 1947, she was blessed with a daughter of her own, whom she named "Beatrice." Margaret remembered her childhood teddy bear and during a visit home, she searched the attic until she found him, wrapped carefully in a blanket and laid carefully in a trunk. She wanted so much to pass this family heirloom on to her a new baby, but poor teddy was even more threadbare and patched than Margaret had remembered. She was about to give up on the plan when her mother came up with an idea. "I think I could knit the little chap a new covering" Mrs. Winston suggested, so teddy was turned over to her for the tender, loving care that only a mother could administer.

Margaret waited patiently and even though the work required many hours of labor, it seemed that teddy was ready to begin his new life within a matter of a week or two. How excited Margaret was when she saw her childhood friend in his brand new covering. Mrs. Winston had painstakingly knitted each limb covering separately so teddy still had movable joints. She carefully made buttonhole openings so teddy's original eyes remained intact.

When Margaret's child, Beatrice, grew too old for teddy, it was again wrapped in a small blanket, but this time it was tucked into the back recesses of the bottom drawer of the dresser in Beatrice's bedroom.

Now the story jumps ahead to the mid 1970s. Beatrice has married and moved away, taking along some of her furnishings, including the dresser. She and her husband decide to replace some of their furniture and an ad placed in the local paper brings an antique dealer to their door the very next day. In the excitement of selling all the furniture to the dealer, poor teddy is carried away with the dresser.

The dealer, who operates a stall at the famous Portobello Road Antique Market in London, discovers the knitted bear while pulling the drawers out to clean the dresser. Knitted teddy bears are not of great value so it is tossed in a box of worn silver and glassware and carted off to the antique market the following Saturday.

This just happened to be the Saturday that we were combing the market for old teddy bears to bring back to the States. Doris was drawn to the knitted bear at once but I tried to talk her out of it. She was determined and teddy made the trip back with us. It was a month or so after our return that Doris discovered the little drawstring holding the knitted covering over teddy's head. She released the knot and pulled back the knitting to bring teddy out of his years of hiding. The knitted covering has been restuffed so it can be displayed along with the well worn, patched and loved teddy that hid inside for all those years.

The Old Man

The old man's bear, 19in (48cm).

My favorite teddy bear in our overgrown collection is a teddy we call "The Old Man's Bear." I am influenced partly because it is an early German bear in a rare cinnamon color, but more importantly because it came from the original owner. He brought the bear to us some ten years ago and it

was obvious from the start that the teddy bear held a very special place in his heart. Let us go back to the beginning to tell the whole story.

Wilhelm Schmidt was born in Vienna, Austria, in 1902. He was the only child of Peter and Freda Schmidt. Peter was a jeweler by trade. Wilhelm's parents were modestly affluent and he wanted for nothing. He was surrounded by many delightful toys made by Germany's finest toy makers in Nüremberg. Wilhelm came from a musical family and in addition to his parents' love of the opera, his Grandfather Schmidt was a violin maker and started young Wilhelm on lessons at the early age of seven.

The boy was not a child prodigy by any means but he was good enough by age ten to enter a local music contest sponsored by the music society. The competition in young Wilhelm's category was strong but in spite of it, he managed to win second place. A beautiful trophy would have been reward enough but his proud grandfather gave Wilhelm a prize that was to be cherished for a lifetime...a magnificent cinnamon teddy bear. The bear was only 19in (48cm) in size but to Wilhelm it was the biggest, most beautiful toy he had ever seen. Some say that by age ten, Wilhelm was really too old for a teddy bear, but he was not intimidated by what others might think and he dearly loved this bear.

Wilhelm had been raised to treat his playthings with respect and his teddy bear was no exception. He would gently lift it down from a shelf in his playroom and after a brief conversation, it was returned to the shelf with the same measure of caution. With his devotion to his teddy bear, it was no surprise that Wilhelm chose teddy over other toys to accompany him and his parents to their new home in America in 1911.

Wilhelm Schmidt now became William Smith and because his parents had the foresight to enroll their son in an English class some months before they left, William made the transition to his new country with relative ease. He was well liked in school, where he participated in the school orchestra. Good grades brought William to a choice between going on to college or taking up his father's trade. Since the business had always been good to his family, William chose to apprentice with his father, who by now had a small jewelry store in central Michigan.

William was very devoted to his family and he spent most of his spare hours looking after the needs of his aging parents. Evenings were spent listening to William play his violin or in talking about their beloved Vienna. Several trips had been made to visit their former home but advancing age

and failing health made it impossible for his parents to travel. William's teddy bear had earned a respected place in a china cabinet in the living room. When the elder Schmidts passed on, within months of each other, William continued to live in the family home and operate the jewelry shop.

William had spent so many years looking after his parents that he was now too old to marry. A neighbor lady who had been widowed two years earlier changed all that, however. William had been fond of his neighbor and within a few years, they became man and wife.

A tragic accident took the life of William's new granddaughter's husband, and they opened their home to the granddaughter and her three young children. It was difficult enough with so many new people to get used to, but William became concerned when his old teddy bear became a plaything for the children. He did not have the heart to take it away but in his mind, he worried about his teddy bear that represented a wonderful childhood. His concerns were amplified when a new puppy joined the family because the dog was fond of tearing up stuffed animals!

One day William made a shopping trip to their local mall, where an antique show was in progress. A teddy bear displayed in one booth caught his eye and he remembered the bear holding a sign that read "Wanted, Old Teddy Bears." After a conversation with his wife that night, William reached a painful decision. The next morning his wife drove him back to the shopping mall with his teddy bear in hand.

We were pleased when this gentleman in his 80s brought his teddy to our booth and when asked if he wanted to sell it, the old man said "nope" and walked away, still holding tightly to his friend. His wife explained that he really wanted to sell us the bear so he could end his nightmares of the dog getting the bear, but he needed just a little more time. She returned in about 30 minutes with the teddy. We learned that several years ago that the old man had passed away. His widow said that although William missed his teddy bear, he mentioned several times that he felt he had made the right decision. William never got to see much of his adopted country but his teddy bear has traveled extensively throughout the United States, where we proudly share it in our traveling museum collection.